Cambridge First Certificate in English 6

Cambridge First Certificate in English 6

Examination papers from University of Cambridge ESOL Examinations: English for Speakers of Other Languages

CAMBRIDGE UNIVERSITY PRESS

PUBLISHED BY THE PRESS SYNDICATE OF THE UNIVERSITY OF CAMBRIDGE
The Pitt Building, Trumpington Street, Cambridge, United Kingdom

CAMBRIDGE UNIVERSITY PRESS
The Edinburgh Building, Cambridge CB2 2RU, UK
40 West 20th Street, New York, NY 10011–4211, USA
477 Williamstown Road, Port Melbourne, VIC 3207, Australia
Ruiz de Alarcón 13, 28014 Madrid, Spain
Dock House, The Waterfront, Cape Town 8001, South Africa

http://www.cambridge.org

First published 2003

Printed in the United Kingdom at the University Press, Cambridge

ISBN 0 521 75443 7   Student's Book
ISBN 0 521 75444 5   Student's Book (with answers)
ISBN 0 521 75446 1   Teacher's Book
ISBN 0 521 75447 X   Set of 2 Cassettes
ISBN 0 521 75448 8   Set of 2 Audio CDs
ISBN 0 521 75445 3   Self-Study pack

Contents

Thanks and acknowledgements

The publishers are grateful to the following for permission to reproduce copyright material. Whilst every effort has been made to locate the owners of copyright, in some cases this has been unsuccessful. The publishers apologise for any infringement or failure to acknowledge the original sources and will be glad to include any necessary correction in subsequent printings.

Times Newspapers for the text on p.3 'Speeding Over Seas' by Jennai Cox from *The Times Wild Spirits Supplement*, 25 April, 1998, for the text on p.55 'Facing the Truth' from the *Brainpower Supplement, The Sunday Times*, February, 1998, and for the text on p.98 'See you in three years says jogger on lap of the world' by Russell Jenkins, *The Times*, 7 December, 1996. © NI Syndication Limited, London; Constable & Robinson Limited for the texts on pp.4 and 30 from *Cross my Heart and Hope to Die* by Sheila Radley, 1992; *The Illustrated London News* for the text on p.9 by Jo Foley, 1998; *New Scientist* magazine for the text on p.29 'The Big Yawn', by Amy Adams, December 1988, © RBI 1988; Mike Bell for the text on p.32 'Living in the Valley' from *Peak and Pennine*, March, 1998; IPC Syndication for the texts on pp.35 and 87 by Nina Hathway, 'Confident people, what's their secret?' from *Woman's Weekly*, February 1997, and 'Variations on a Theme' from *Woman's Weekly*, July, 1996, © Nina Hathway/*Woman's Weekly*/IPC Syndication; *The Independent* for the text on p.56 'The Shell Artist' by Peter Cooke, 27 April, 1996, and for the text on p.82 'Film Critic' by Mark Adams, 11 October, 1996; the Editor of *Caterer & Hotelkeeper* for the text on p.58 from the article 'Chips with everything', 29 January, 1998; New Holland Publishers (UK) Limited for the adapted text on p.72 from *Secret London* by Andrew Duncan, 1995; Rose Rouse for the text on p.84 from the article 'Fun at the Dentist's, *The Guardian*, 31 December, 1996.

For permission to reproduce copyright photographs:

Art Directors & TRIP/C Kapolka for p.32, /J Greenberg for p.C1 (bottom), /Helene Rogers for p.C6 (top left), /J Stanley for p.13 (top), /B Gadsby for p.13 (bottom), /S Grant for p.C16 (top); John Birdsall Photography for pp.C5 (bottom), C12 (bottom),

C15 (bottom left); Getty Images/Stewart Cohen for p.C5 (top), Don Johnston for p.C7 (top), /John Warden for p.C7 (centre), /Alan Klehr for p.C8 (top), /E Dygas for p.C8 (bottom), /Howard Kingsnorth for p.C9 (top), /Andy Caulfield for p.C9 (bottom), /Chris Ladd for p.C14 (top), /Daniel Pangbourne for p.C14 (centre), /Justin Pumfrey for p.C14 (bottom), /VCL/Alistair Berg for p.C15 (top right); Sally & Richard Greenhill Photo Library/Sally Greenhill for p.C1 (top), /Richard Greenhill for pp.C6 (bottom right), C16 (bottom); Robert Harding Picture Library/Dr Müller for p.C12 (top); Life File Photographic Library/Emma Lee for p.C6 (bottom left), /Angela Maynard for p.C15 (bottom right); W Lloyd Jerome for p.84; The Merrion Hotel, Dublin for p.58; Pictures Colour Library for p.C4 (top), p.C4 (bottom), and p.C7 (bottom); Sporting Pictures (UK)/Jardine for p.C6 (top right); <http://www.shoutpictures.com/>www.shoutpictures.com for p.C15 (top left).

Artwork: Oxford Designers & Illustrators

Picture research by Valerie Mulcahy

Text permissions by Jean Kennedy

Design concept by Peter Ducker

Cover design by Dunne & Scully

The recordings which accompany this book were made at Studio AVP, London

To the student

This book is for candidates preparing for the University of Cambridge ESOL Examinations First Certificate in English (FCE). The FCE examination is widely recognised in commerce and industry and in individual university faculties and other educational institutions.

The collection of four complete practice tests comprises past papers from the Cambridge First Certificate in English examination; you can practise these tests on your own or with the help of your teacher.

The FCE examination is part of a group of examinations developed by Cambridge ESOL called the Cambridge Main Suite. The Main Suite consists of five examinations that have similar characteristics but are designed for different levels of English language ability. Within the five levels, FCE is at Cambridge/ALTE Level 3, Level B2 in the Council of Europe Framework and Level 1 in the UK National Qualifications Framework.

Examination	Cambridge/ALTE Level	Council of Europe Framework Level	UK National Qualifications Framework Level
CPE Certificate of Proficiency in English	Level 5	C2	3
CAE Certificate in Advanced English	Level 4	C1	2
FCE First Certificate in English	Level 3	B2	1
PET Preliminary English Test	Level 2	B1	Entry 3
KET Key English Test	Level 1	A2	Entry 2
YLE Cambridge Young Learners English	Breakthrough Level		

The FCE examination consists of five papers:

Paper 1	**Reading**	1 hour 15 minutes
Paper 2	**Writing**	1 hour 30 minutes
Paper 3	**Use of English**	1 hour 15 minutes
Paper 4	**Listening**	40 minutes (approximately)
Paper 5	**Speaking**	14 minutes

Paper 1   Reading

This paper consists of **four parts**. Each part contains a text and some questions. Part 4 may contain two or more shorter related texts. There are **35 questions** in total, including multiple choice, gapped text and matching questions.

Paper 2   Writing

This paper consists of **two parts**. For both parts you have to write between 120 and 180 words. Part 1 is **compulsory**. It provides texts which are sometimes accompanied by visual material to help you write a letter.

In Part 2, there are four tasks from which you **choose one** to write about. The range of tasks from which questions may be drawn includes an article, a report, a composition, a short story and a letter. The last question is based on the set books. These books remain on the list for about two years and you should contact Cambridge ESOL, or the Cambridge ESOL Local Secretary in your area, if you wish to have the up-to-date list of set books. If you decide to do the question on the set books, there will be two options from which you can **choose one** to write about.

Paper 3   Use of English

This paper consists of **five parts** and tests your control of English grammar, vocabulary and spelling. There are **65 questions** in total. The tasks include gap-filling exercises, sentence transformation, word formation and error correction.

Paper 4   Listening

This paper contains **four parts**. Each part contains a recorded text or texts and some questions including multiple choice, note-taking, sentence completion and matching. You hear each text twice. There is a total of **30 questions**.

Paper 5   Speaking

This paper consists of **four parts**. The standard test format is two candidates and two examiners. One examiner takes part in the conversation, the other examiner listens and gives marks. You will be given photographs and other visual material to look at and talk about. Sometimes you will talk with the other candidate, sometimes with the examiner and sometimes with both.

Marks and results

Your overall FCE grade is based on the total score gained in all five papers. It is not necessary to achieve a satisfactory level in all five papers in order to pass the examination. Certificates are given to candidates who pass the examination with grade A, B or C. A is the highest. The minimum successful performance in order to achieve a grade C corresponds to about 60% of the total marks. D and E are failing grades. Your Statement of Results will include a graphical profile of your performance in each paper and show your relative performance in each one. Each paper is weighted to 40 marks. Therefore, the five FCE papers total 200 marks, after weighting.

Further information

For more information about FCE or any other Cambridge ESOL examination write to:

University of Cambridge
ESOL Examinations
1 Hills Road
Cambridge
CB1 2EU
England

Telephone: +44 1223 553355
Fax: +44 1223 460278
e-mail: ESOLHelpdesk@ucles.org.uk
www.CambridgeESOL.org

In some areas this information can also be obtained from the British Council.

Test 1

PAPER 1   READING (1 hour 15 minutes)

Part 1

You are going to read a magazine article about personal watercraft – also known as 'jet-skis'. Choose from the list **A-I** the sentence which best summarises each part (**1-7**) of the article. There is one extra sentence which you do not need to use. There is an example at the beginning (**0**).

Mark your answers **on the separate answer sheet**.

A   Personal watercraft are now regarded as having a more serious role.

B   There is now greater emphasis on the correct way of using personal watercraft.

C   Personal watercraft are likely to grow in popularity in the future.

D   Personal watercraft have changed because the kind of people using them has changed.

E   The majority of people using personal watercraft do so because it is enjoyable.

F   Personal watercraft used to have a terrible reputation.

G   Personal watercraft enable you to experience travelling on the sea in relative comfort.

H   The reason why people like using personal watercraft has changed.

I   Personal watercraft enable you to combine opposing wishes.

SPEEDING OVER SEAS

Jennai Cox reports on riding the ocean waves on personal watercraft.

0 ┃ **I**

If you like the water but are not keen on getting wet; if you enjoy speed but without the associated risks; if you like to keep active but prefer not to make too much effort; and if you have given up all hope of finding a sport that will accommodate your conflicting preferences, think again. Think personal watercraft.

1

When the sport rose to popularity in Britain a few years ago, it was, like many thrilling new activities, taken up by young risk-takers. It became known as jet-skiing and before long was given a very bad name. The noise, the antics and, inevitably, the accidents caused by this unregulated sport annoyed anglers, sailors and swimmers alike.

2

Having exhausted the number of thrills they could get from their personal watercraft, many of the younger sensation-seekers are moving on to more challenging activities. Left to the more mature in mind and years, the sport has been forced to grow up. Now that the average age of those purchasing personal watercraft is 42, and a growing percentage of the market is made up of families, the machines have had to adapt: two- and three-seater personal watercraft are becoming the norm.

3

Mindful of past criticism, personal watercraft manufacturers are trying to ensure that all owners, especially the new ones, are taught seamanship, navigation and harbour rules. The machines are now registered and should be sold with a safety handbook and video, as well as an operator's guide.

4

As with so many other powerful machines, it is not the vehicle that causes danger but the person driving it. But now that personal watercraft are becoming larger, more sophisticated and able to hold more fuel, the attraction has changed from danger to distance. More and more personal watercraft users today want to cruise.

5

Riding on personal watercraft is like taking a civilised rollercoaster ride on water. Because you are so close to the elements, you feel more a part of them, without having to put up with their more unpleasant aspects. Apart from the odd splash, and wet feet, you stay comparatively dry and are much more able to enjoy the delights of being at sea.

6

Having overcome hostility, personal watercraft and their users are gradually being seen in a more positive light. Despite being rich people's toys – they can cost several thousand pounds – their capabilities as lifeboat vehicles are beginning to be developed. Quick and easy to launch, they can reach swimmers who are in trouble or the shipwrecked very swiftly and, being so easy to manoeuvre, can be driven closer than many boats. A stretcher which can be pulled behind has also recently been developed.

7

To drive personal watercraft safely at speed requires skill, agility, endurance and arm strength. But the basics are easy. The disabled have discovered that personal watercraft allow them to take part in a sport without feeling at a disadvantage. And for most people discovering personal watercraft, pursuing a competitive or fitness-improving activity is not the idea. Pleasure is the goal and most of them achieve it.

Part 2

You are going to read an extract from a novel. For questions **8-14**, choose the answer
(**A**, **B**, **C** or **D**) which you think fits best according to the text.

Mark your answers **on the separate answer sheet**.

Many trees in the Brackham area were brought down in the terrible storms that March. The town itself lost two great lime trees from the former market square. The disappearance of such prominent features had altered the appearance of the town centre entirely, to the annoyance of its more conservative inhabitants.

Among the annoyed, under more normal circumstances, would have been Chief Inspector Douglas Pelham, head of the local police force. But at the height of that week's storm, when the wind brought down even the mature walnut tree in his garden, Pelham had in fact been in no fit state to notice. A large and healthy man, he had for the first time in his life been seriously ill with an attack of bronchitis.

When he first complained of an aching head and tightness in his chest, his wife, Molly, had tried to persuade him to go to the doctor. Convinced that the police force could not do without him, he had, as usual, ignored her and attempted to carry on working. Predictably, though he wouldn't have listened to anyone who tried to tell him so, this had the effect of fogging his memory and shortening his temper.

It was only when his colleague, Sergeant Lloyd, took the initiative and drove him to the doctor's door that he finally gave in. By that time, he didn't have the strength left to argue with
17 her. In no time at all, she was taking him along to the chemist's to get his prescribed antibiotics and then home to his unsurprised wife who sent him straight to bed.

When Molly told him, on the Thursday morning, that the walnut tree had been brought down during the night, Pelham hadn't been able to take it in. On Thursday evening, he had asked weakly about damage to the house, groaned thankfully when he heard there was none, and pulled the sheets over his head.

It wasn't until Saturday, when the antibiotics took effect, his temperature dropped and he got up, that he realised with a shock that the loss of the walnut tree had made a permanent difference to the appearance of the living-room. The Pelhams' large house stood in a sizeable garden. It had not come cheap, but even so Pelham had no regrets about buying it. The leafy garden had created an impression of privacy. Now, though, the storm had changed his outlook. Previously the view from the living-room had featured the handsome walnut tree. This had not darkened the room because there was also a window on the opposite wall, but it had provided interesting patterns of light and shade that disguised the true state of the worn furniture that the family had brought with them from their previous house.

With the tree gone, the room seemed cruelly bright, its worn furnishings exposed in all their
33 shabbiness. And the view from the window didn't bear looking at. The tall house next door, previously hidden by the tree, was now there, dominating the outlook with its unattractive purple bricks and external pipes. It seemed to have a great many upstairs windows, all of them watching the Pelhams' every movement.

'Doesn't it look terrible?' Pelham croaked to his wife.

But Molly, standing in the doorway, sounded more pleased than dismayed. 'That's what I've been telling you ever since we came here. We have to buy a new sofa, whatever it costs.'

8   Why were some people in Brackham annoyed after the storm?

  A   The town looked different.
  B   The police had done little to help.
  C   No market could be held.
  D   Fallen trees had not been removed.

9   Who does 'her' in line 17 refer to?

  A   Molly Pelham
  B   the doctor
  C   Sergeant Lloyd
  D   the chemist

10   When Chief Inspector Pelham's wife first told him about the walnut tree, he appeared to be

  A   worried.
  B   shocked.
  C   saddened.
  D   uninterested.

11   What aspect of the Pelhams' furniture does 'shabbiness' in line 33 describe?

  A   its colour
  B   its condition
  C   its position
  D   its design

12   As a result of the storm, the Pelhams' living-room

  A   was pleasantly lighter.
  B   felt less private.
  C   had a better view.
  D   was in need of repair.

13   Why did Molly sound pleased by her husband's comment?

  A   It proved that he was well again.
  B   She agreed about the tree.
  C   She thought he meant the sofa.
  D   It was what she expected him to say.

14   From what we learn of Chief Inspector Pelham, he could best be described as

  A   open-minded.
  B   well-liked.
  C   warm-hearted.
  D   strong-willed.

Part 3

You are going to read a magazine article about country music star Pam Tillis. Eight paragraphs have been removed from the article. Choose from the paragraphs **A-I** the one which fits each gap (**15-21**). There is one extra paragraph which you do not need to use. There is an example at the beginning (**0**).

Mark your answers **on the separate answer sheet**.

Wild Angel

Country music star Pam Tillis talks about her life and work.

While in the studio recording her album *All Of This Love*, country music star Pam Tillis found herself imagining an old dance hall. As a result, the Mexican-flavoured ballad, 'Tequila Mockingbird', one of the album's highlights, is punctuated by the sound of her dance steps.

0	I

The eldest child of famed country singer Mel Tillis, Pam has been in the business long enough to know when to add something a little unusual to her music. But far from being the 'golden child' with a one-way ticket to success, Pam Tillis's journey to stardom has been full of ups and downs.

15	

Then her life was turned upside down. At the age of 16, Pam was involved in a serious car accident, leading to years of plastic surgery and occasional pain ever since.

16	

After the accident, she attended the University of Tennessee, and it was here that Pam started her first band. Leaving college in 1976, she worked for a time in her father's publishing company, Sawgrass Music, but then it was time to leave the nest.

17	

In the late 1970s, this area was a magnet for young Americans. There was no better place to be, and

Pam's new friends there encouraged her to widen her musical tastes.

18	

'It was a crazy time,' Pam recalls. 'When you're young, you go any way the wind blows, so I was experimenting and seeing what I could do. I was searching for my identity, if you like.'

19	

Returning to Nashville in 1978, Pam was still looking for her place. Some of her songs had been recorded by other artists, but she now began the search for her first recording contract.

20	

The rest, as they say, is history. Recently voted Female Singer of the Year by the Country Music Association, and with a series of best-selling records behind her, the most difficult part of Pam's life these days is balancing her home life, with her husband and young son, and her career.

21	

'In some ways it was worse in Dad's day,' admits Pam. 'There was no TV or video and they were away 100 days or more a year. But the sacrifice is worth it. It's a way of teaching your kids about having a dream, and how important it is to follow that dream.'

A However, this took longer than she expected, and having a famous father didn't automatically open doors. She sang in a rhythm and blues band, and after five years of writing and singing, finally got her big chance.

B Pam enjoyed playing with the group she had formed. 'There's enormous energy out there,' she states emphatically. 'I lasted just over a year, but then it was time to go home.'

C Pam first appeared on a major stage at the age of eight, singing with her father. As a teenager, she showed up at many talent nights in Nashville, and performed at local clubs.

D Pam, however, produced her latest record herself. 'It was rewarding and enjoyable,' she says, 'but I wish I'd been able to take a whole year over it.'

E California has always been the destination for America's hopefuls and dreamers. Pam felt limited by life in Nashville, and so she too moved to the west coast.

F However, having the advantage of growing up in the music business herself, Pam knows what this involves. She understands what is necessary in terms of hard work and lonely nights spent in hotel rooms.

G Pam believes that the experience gave her a greater determination to live the life she wanted. 'If something dramatic like that happens to anyone, it makes them think they survived for a reason.'

H One in particular told her that she was capable of singing any kind of music she wanted. Keen to spread her artistic wings, she put together a 'loose jazz/rock band' called Freelight.

I 'It wasn't planned. My violin player started to play his solo and my mind was transported to a time about 200 years ago. When I started dancing, the noise seemed so appropriate that we left it on the record.'

Part 4

You are going to read a magazine article about five young designers. For questions **22-35**, choose from the designers (**A-E**). The designers may be chosen more than once. When more than one answer is required, these may be given in any order. There is an example at the beginning (**0**).

Mark your answers **on the separate answer sheet**.

Which designer(s)

works in a variety of environments?	**0** C	
advises against certain styles?	**22**	
says they took a business decision based on their own personal taste?	**23**	
had begun designing before being trained?	**24**	
have adapted a traditional style?	**25**	**26**
is working with a material which is new to them?	**27**	
have used their reputation to develop a new area of business?	**28**	**29**
are completely self-taught?	**30**	**31**
mention how tastes have changed recently?	**32**	**33**
have received professional recognition?	**34**	**35**

Style Merchants

Style informs every part of our lives today from clothes to interior decoration and accessories. Jo Foley provides a taste of the trends for this year's followers of fashion.

A   Ned Ingham: Dress Designer

Ned Ingham makes dreamy, romantic wedding dresses. 'People are turning away from the traditional, rather stiff dresses to much simpler styles,' he explains. Ingham has been drawing and designing wedding dresses since he was a schoolboy. Then, at the age of 16, he enrolled at fashion school, where he gained the technical skills to cut and construct clothes. But you do not have to be a bride to own an Ingham dress: he also designs long, classic evening dresses, given a fresh touch by up-to-the-minute colours and fabrics. For the less adventurous, Ingham's designs include a classical summer navy-blue suit, the centrepiece of the Englishwoman's wardrobe for most of the 20th century. But in his hands, it looks as new as tomorrow.

B   Sally Quail: Jeweller

Although she once worked for an art dealer, Sally Quail has had no formal training in jewellery. It was only when she could not find an engagement ring she liked that she decided to design her own. The resulting enquiries encouraged her to set up as a designer in 1990. Now her pieces are sought out by many stars of stage and screen. Her signature style is large semi-precious stones set in gold to make magnificent necklaces, bracelets and rings fashioned after those worn in the 18th century. However, she has recently begun to use the most precious stone of all – diamonds. 'It must reflect my age,' says 36-year-old Quail. 'I reached that moment in every woman's life when she wants a diamond and that is when I began working with them.'

C   Penny Pratt: Florist

In addition to running her tiny shop, Penny Pratt is a flower consultant for a large chain of supermarkets and provides floral ideas to a number of top restaurants. All of this is good going for someone who has no floristry qualifications and gave up her job as a teacher 10 years ago in order to do 'something different'. And her simple, yet incredibly modern, creations have begun to capture every design prize in the flower business, which has helped her in setting up her own London Flower School. She has recently combined her skills on extremely successful lecture trips to Japan and the USA. She says, 'Flower arrangements are much simpler these days. Keep them simple but strong and don't have too many leaves – they are too large and architectural. For wedding bouquets, whatever your arrangement, the golden rule remains the flowers must be of the same species.'

D   Peter Little: Hairdresser

For over 20 years, Peter Little has taken his scissors to some of the world's top heads. Everyone who is anyone has had their hair styled by this man. 'Most women want real-looking hair and a style they can manage at home,' he says. So his approach is a novel one – to ensure that his clients never appear as if they have just walked out of a salon. But this carefree attitude and casual look does not come cheap – £250 for the first appointment, and there's a three-month waiting list. Trading on his celebrity, Peter has produced his own range of hairdryers and other styling equipment. Now, those who can't make it to his salon can create their own styles back at home.

E   Lily Grimson: Handbag Designer

Just four years after setting up in the fiercely competitive fashion business, Lily Grimson, with only an introductory course in art and design behind her, has had two of her creations selected for a major design exhibition. Whatever the shape and form of her designs, they are never ignored. All of Grimson's fashion bags are handmade in the UK. The Grimson handbag is not simply a container – the bags are full of glamour, whether fashioned from the finest calfskin or the heaviest silk. A combination of chic and care make a Grimson bag something special.

PAPER 2   WRITING (1 hour 30 minutes)

Part 1

You **must** answer this question.

1   You ordered a gift by post for a friend's birthday. The company were late sending the gift to you and you were also not happy with it. Below is the advertisement for the gift, on which you have written some notes.

Read the advertisement, together with your notes. Then, using all the information in your notes, write a **letter** to Mr P. Marsden of Personal Pens Limited. You should explain why you are not happy with the gift and ask for your money back.

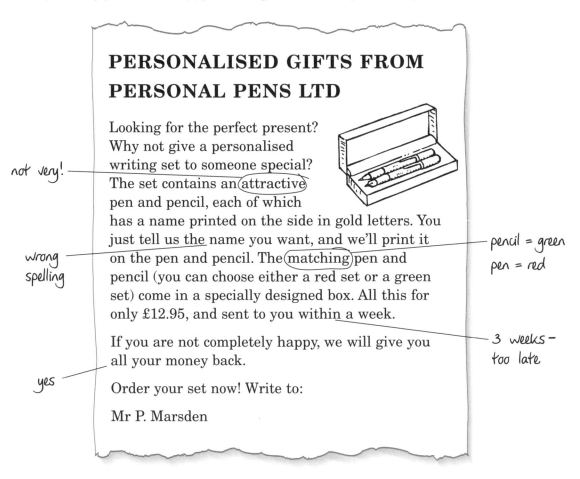

Write a **letter** of between **120** and **180** words in an appropriate style on the opposite page. Do not write any postal addresses.

Question 1

....

....

....

....

....

....

....

....

....

....

....

....

....

....

....

....

....

....

....

....

....

....

....

....

....

....

....

....

....

....

....

....

Part 2

Write an answer to **one** of the questions **2-5** in this part. Write your answer in **120-180** words in an appropriate style on the opposite page. Put the question number in the box.

2   You have had a class discussion on fashion. Your teacher has now asked you to write a composition, giving your opinions on the following statement:

Young people always want to dress differently from their parents.

Write your **composition**.

3   You see this announcement in your school magazine.

> ## *New Clubs after School*
>
> *Your school wants to start some new after-school clubs. Chess, table tennis, guitar playing and cookery have been suggested as possible ideas for clubs. What do you think? Write us an article for the school magazine covering the points below.*
>
> *   *Tell us which **one** of these four ideas you like best **and** why.*
> *   *Make **one** other suggestion for a new club **and** explain why it would be a good idea.*

Write your **article**.

4   The local tourist office has asked you to write a report on interesting things for visitors to see and do on a **one-day** sightseeing tour of your area. In your report, include suggestions about where visitors should go and what they should do in order to spend an interesting day in your area.

Write your **report**.

5   Answer **one** of the following two questions based on your reading of **one** of these set books. Write (**a**) or (**b**) as well as the number **5** in the question box, and the **title** of the book next to the box. Your answer **must** be about one of the books below.

Best Detective Stories of Agatha Christie – Longman Fiction
The Old Man and the Sea – Ernest Hemingway
A Window on the Universe – Oxford Bookworms Collection
Cry Freedom – John Briley
Wuthering Heights – Emily Brontë

Either   (**a**)   You have had a class discussion on whether the characters in the book or short story you have read are believable. Your teacher has now asked you to write a composition on this subject. Write your **composition**, explaining your views with reference to the book or one of the short stories you have read.

Or   (**b**)   An English-speaking friend is going on a long journey soon and has asked you to recommend a book to read during the journey. Write a **letter** to your friend, giving some information about the book or short stories you have read. You should give reasons for your recommendation.

Question

....

....

....

....

....

....

....

....

....

....

....

....

....

....

....

....

....

....

....

....

....

....

....

....

....

....

....

....

PAPER 3   USE OF ENGLISH (1 hour 15 minutes)

Part 1

For questions **1-15**, read the text below and decide which answer (**A**, **B**, **C** or **D**) best fits each space. There is an example at the beginning (**0**).

Mark your answers **on the separate answer sheet**.

Example:

0 **A** learn   **B** capture   **C** discover   **D** get

0	A	B	C	D

LEARNING TO MAKE A PERFECT PIZZA

According to the European Pizza-Makers' Association, making a good pizza is not a straightforward skill to **(0)** ..... . The ingredients seem very **(1)** ..... : flour, yeast, water and a bit of salt. But water and flour can easily **(2)** ..... glue and anyone who has eaten a **(3)** ..... quality pizza will know how bad it can make your stomach **(4)** ..... .

'In Italy, 70 per cent of pizza makers could improve on their product, not to **(5)** ..... all the pizza makers around the world who **(6)** ..... uneatable meals,' says Antonio Primiceri, the Association's founder. He has now started a pizza school in an attempt to **(7)** ..... the reputation of this traditional dish. As part of an **(8)** ..... course, the students at Mr Primiceri's school are taught to **(9)** ..... common mistakes, produce a good basic mixture, add a tasty topping and cook the pizza properly. 'Test the finished pizza by breaking the crust,' advises Mr Primiceri. 'If the soft **(10)** ..... inside the pizza is white, clean and dry, it's a good pizza. If it is not like this, the pizza will **(11)** ..... your stomach. You will feel **(12)** ..... full and also thirsty.'

In Italy alone, the pizza **(13)** ..... has an annual turnover of more than $12 billion. Mr Primiceri **(14)** ..... that there are 10,000 jobs in pizza restaurants waiting to be **(15)** ..... by those with real skill. 'If you are a good pizza cook, you will never be without a job,' he says.

1 **A** simple   **B** primary   **C** pure   **D** regular

2 **A** mix   **B** construct   **C** assemble   **D** make

3 **A** sad   **B** poor   **C** short   **D** weak

4 **A** sense   **B** do   **C** feel   **D** be

5 **A** state   **B** mention   **C** remark   **D** tell

6 **A** submit   **B** give   **C** serve   **D** deal

7 **A** save   **B** provide   **C** deliver   **D** return

8 **A** extensive   **B** extreme   **C** intensive   **D** intentional

9 **A** pass   **B** escape   **C** miss   **D** avoid

10 **A** spot   **B** part   **C** side   **D** slice

11 **A** worry   **B** upset   **C** ache   **D** depress

12 **A** hardly   **B** tightly   **C** uncomfortably   **D** heavily

13 **A** activity   **B** body   **C** industry   **D** company

14 **A** computes   **B** estimates   **C** assesses   **D** counts

15 **A** employed   **B** filled   **C** completed   **D** covered

Part 2

For questions **16-30**, read the text below and think of the word which best fits each space. Use only **one** word in each space. There is an example at the beginning (**0**). Write your answers **on the separate answer sheet**.

Example: | **0** | *it* |

HOLLYWOOD

How was **(0)** ....*it*.... that Hollywood came to be the place everyone associates with the American film industry? It's a strange story.

There was a little village in southern California called Cahuenga Valley **(16)** .... a Mr and Mrs Wilcox had their home. In 1887, **(17)** .... Mrs Wilcox was on a trip to the east coast, she got into conversation **(18)** .... a stranger on a train. The stranger had a home called Hollywood somewhere else in the country, **(19)** .... Mrs Wilcox liked the name **(20)** .... much that she decided to give her home the same name. Because the Wilcox's home was the biggest in Cahuenga Valley, the village soon became known **(21)** .... Hollywood.

In normal circumstances most people **(22)** .... never have heard of Hollywood. However, between 1908 and 1913 **(23)** .... else happened. Many small independent film companies began moving to southern California **(24)** .... two main reasons. Firstly, they were attracted by the sunny climate, which let them film throughout the year **(25)** .... the need for expensive lighting. Secondly, they were **(26)** .... problems with the larger, more powerful studios in New York, and they wanted to get away from there.

Only one studio actually set **(27)** .... in Hollywood. Local people were so angry when it appeared that **(28)** .... law was passed forbidding the building of any more studios. In fact, Hollywood itself never had a film industry, surprisingly enough, **(29)** .... the other studios that came to the area were all built outside Hollywood. Nevertheless, by 1915 'Hollywood' **(30)** .... become familiar as a term for the movie business as a whole.

Part 3

For questions **31-40**, complete the second sentence so that it has a similar meaning to the first sentence, using the word given. **Do not change the word given**. You must use between **two** and **five** words, including the word given.

Here is an example (**0**).

Example:

0   You must do exactly what the manager tells you.

    carry

    You must ……………………….......…………. instructions exactly.

The gap can be filled by the words 'carry out the manager's' so you write:

0	carry out the manager's

Write **only the missing words** on the separate answer sheet.

---

31   So that John could go on holiday in the summer, he saved £10 a week.

    order

    John saved £10 a week ……………………………………………… able to go on holiday in the summer.

32   It's not worth asking the manager for the day off.

    point

    There …………………………………………… in asking the manager for the day off.

33   We had to finish all the work before we could leave.

    until

    We had to stay …………………………………………… all the work.

34   Tim had not expected the concert to be so good.

    better

    The concert …………………………………………… had expected.

35 If Cheryl doesn't train harder, she'll never get into the swimming team.

does

Cheryl will never get into the swimming team ....
more training.

36 'Do you realise what the time is, Steve?' asked Chris.

what

Chris asked Steve .... it was.

37 The company decided to advertise the job in a national newspaper.

put

The company decided to .... the job in a
national newspaper.

38 At the end of his speech, the winner thanked his parents.

finished

The winner .... his parents.

39 I applied for the job a month ago.

month

It .... I applied for the job.

40 They received many letters of support after they had appeared on television.

following

They received many letters of support ....
on television.

Part 4

For questions **41-55**, read the text below and look carefully at each line. Some of the lines are correct, and some have a word which should not be there.

If a line is correct, put a tick (✓) by the number **on the separate answer sheet**. If a line has a word which should **not** be there, write the word **on the separate answer sheet**. There are two examples at the beginning (**0** and **00**).

Examples:

0	✓
00	*me*

TAKING BETTER PHOTOGRAPHS

0	Like many people, I have had a camera for almost as long as I can
00	remember, and I have always enjoyed me taking photographs of
41	my family and friends, and places I have been visited. Then, about a year
42	ago, I noticed that most of the photos I was so proud of which were in
43	fact all very similar to each other. They all showed groups of people
44	standing by a famous building or some other attraction. You hardly
45	couldn't make out their faces clearly, and so it was difficult to get
46	an idea of how had everybody felt. I was looking for a new hobby at
47	the time, and have decided that I would start taking photography
48	more seriously. I thought it would be expensive, but, after reading
49	a few chapters of a book I borrowed from a friend, I last realised that
50	I could improve a great deal extra without spending a lot of money on new
51	equipment. Soon, instead of just taking out the same old pictures, I
52	was photographing those trees, animals, people I didn't know and so
53	on. This soon made a real difference to the quality of my photographs
54	as I began to concentrate myself on getting the best picture possible. I
55	am pleased with the results because I have achieved in such a short time.

Part 5

For questions **56-65**, read the text below. Use the word given in capitals at the end of each line to form a word that fits in the space in the same line. There is an example at the beginning (**0**). Write your answers **on the separate answer sheet**.

Example: | **0** | *meeting* |

A NEW SUPERMARKET FOR THE TOWN

At a (**0**) ..*meeting*. held in Oxwell last Thursday evening a wide	**MEET**
(**56**) ..... of opinions was expressed on plans to build a large	**VARY**
supermarket in the town. A (**57**) ..... of the supermarket group	**DIRECT**
stated that the supermarket would benefit the (**58**) ..... of	**INHABIT**
Oxwell as it would give people more (**59**) ..... when shopping	**CHOOSE**
and would lead to a (**60**) ..... in the number of jobs available in	**GROW**
the town, which has a high rate of (**61**) ..... . Although there was	**EMPLOY**
(**62**) ..... on the need for new jobs, some of those present	**AGREE**
claimed that the supermarket would lead to a (**63**) ..... of jobs as	**LOSE**
small shops, (**64**) ..... to compete with supermarket prices,	**ABLE**
would be forced to close. The final (**65**) ..... on whether or	**DECIDE**
not to build the supermarket will be made next month.	

PAPER 4   LISTENING (approximately 40 minutes)

Part 1

You will hear people talking in eight different situations. For questions **1-8**, choose the best answer (**A**, **B** or **C**).

---

1 You hear part of a radio play.
   Where is the scene taking place?

   A   in the street

   B   in a bank

   C   in a police station

2 You overhear the beginning of a lecture.
   What subject are the students taking?

   A   medicine

   B   sport

   C   music

3 You overhear a conversation in a college.
   Who is the young man?

   A   a new student

   B   a student in the middle of a course

   C   a former student

4 You hear a woman on the radio talking about a cookbook.
   What does she regret?

   A   not looking after it

   B   not having kept it

   C   not using it properly

5 You hear someone talking about the day he met someone famous.
How did he feel after meeting Chris Turner?

    A   unimpressed with the footballer

    B   angry with his friend

    C   disappointed with himself

6 You hear a woman talking on the phone.
Why has she called?

    A   to request a meeting

    B   to offer assistance

    C   to apologise for her absence

7 You overhear an extract from a radio play.
What is the young woman's relationship with the man?

    A   She's a pupil of his.

    B   She's a relative of his.

    C   She's a patient of his.

8 You hear someone telling a story about a strange thing that
happened in the mountains.
What point does the story prove?

    A   how strange things can be explained simply

    B   how easy it is to imagine things

    C   how you can be tricked by the silence

Part 2

You will hear part of a talk about dolls. For questions **9-18**, complete the sentences.

The first known dolls were found in [**9**] in ancient Egypt.

The earliest dolls in the museum date from the [**10**]

Early European dolls were dressed like [**11**]

On the 17th-century dolls, you can see details like the [**12**]

17th-century dolls may cost as much as [**13**] each.

Collectors look for examples in perfect condition, with their [**14**]

19th-century dolls had [**15**] and real hair.

If you can take off the doll's hair, you may see the

[**16**] underneath.

Before the 20th-century, all dolls were [**17**] , not babies.

From the 1930s, dolls were made of [**18**]

Part 3

You will hear five different people talking about why they decided to become nurses. For questions **19-23**, choose which of the reasons (**A-F**) each speaker is giving. Use the letters only once. There is one extra letter which you do not need to use.

A It was a childhood dream.

Speaker 1	19

B Teachers had recommended it.

Speaker 2	20

C A friend had decided to do it.

Speaker 3	21

D It offered a secure income.

Speaker 4	22

E It is a family tradition.

Speaker 5	23

F It is emotionally satisfying.

Part 4

You will hear part of a radio programme in which a book critic gives information about three new books on the subject of travelling in the United States of America. For questions **24-30**, decide which book each statement refers to. Write **A** for **A to Z**,
J for **Just Go** or
TT for **Travel Treat**.

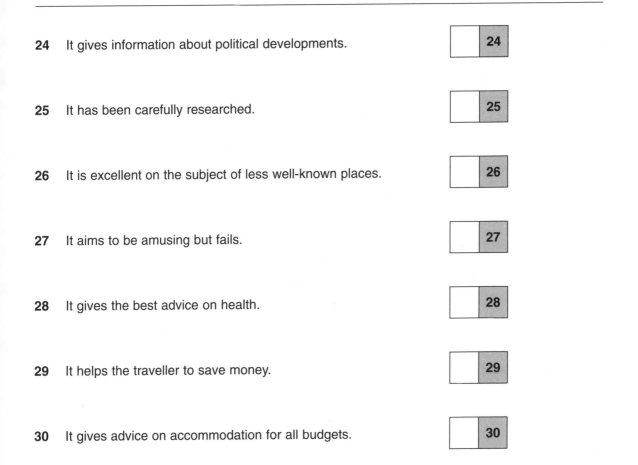

24   It gives information about political developments.   24

25   It has been carefully researched.   25

26   It is excellent on the subject of less well-known places.   26

27   It aims to be amusing but fails.   27

28   It gives the best advice on health.   28

29   It helps the traveller to save money.   29

30   It gives advice on accommodation for all budgets.   30

PAPER 5   SPEAKING (14 minutes)

You take the Speaking test with another candidate, referred to here as your partner. There are two examiners. One will speak to you and your partner and the other will be listening. Both examiners will award marks.

Part 1 (3 minutes)

The examiner asks you and your partner questions about yourselves. You may be asked about things like 'your home town', 'your interests', 'your career plans', etc.

Part 2 (4 minutes)

The examiner gives you two photographs and asks you to talk about them for one minute. The examiner then asks your partner a question about your photographs and your partner responds briefly.

Then the examiner gives your partner two different photographs. Your partner talks about these photographs for one minute. This time the examiner asks you a question about your partner's photographs and you respond briefly.

Part 3 (approximately 3 minutes)

The examiner asks you and your partner to talk together. You may be asked to solve a problem or try to come to a decision about something. For example, you might be asked to decide the best way to use some rooms in a language school. The examiner gives you a picture to help you but does not join in the conversation.

Part 4 (approximately 4 minutes)

The examiner joins in the conversation. You all talk together in a more general way about what has been said in Part 3. The examiner asks you questions but you and your partner are also expected to develop the conversation.

Test 2

PAPER 1   READING (1 hour 15 minutes)

Part 1

You are going to read an article about research into yawning. Choose from the list **A-I** the most suitable heading for each part (**1-7**) of the article. There is one extra heading which you do not need to use. There is an example at the beginning (**0**).

Mark your answers **on the separate answer sheet**.

A   An aid to achievement

B   Failure to prove a theory

C   A way to send people to sleep

D   Losing the battle

E   Questioning a widespread belief

F   Results which support a theory

G   Not widely researched

H   A partly explained theory

I   Behaviour that spreads quickly

Yawning

0	I

When one person yawns in a room, other people begin to yawn. Yawning is contagious, and once you start, there is almost nothing you can do to stop. Of course, the big question is: why do we yawn at all? What possible advantage can there be in keeping our mouths wide open for several seconds? Is it a need for oxygen? Too much carbon dioxide in the blood? Time for bed?

1	

It is none of these according to Robert Provine, an American psychologist. Provine first became curious about yawning when he realised that nobody had really studied this extremely common aspect of behaviour. 'Most scientists are looking for the deep and obscure,' Provine says. 'I look for the significance of everyday behaviour that people have neglected.' With this in mind, he and several other psychologists decided to find out when, why and how we yawn.

2	

Conventional wisdom has long held that we yawn in order to wake up our weary brains with a refreshing burst of oxygen. Assuming that this is true, Provine reasoned, then people who are running low on oxygen – or high on carbon dioxide – should yawn more often than normal. To find out if this was the case, Provine first had to try to make people yawn more.

3	

In his laboratory, Provine gathered together a group of students and told them to think about yawning while they breathed in mixtures of air that were either high in oxygen, high in carbon dioxide or completely normal. Although the gases made the students breathe faster, none of the different gases altered the students' rate of yawning, which held steady at about 24 yawns an hour. Exercise, which also speeds up breathing, made no difference to the yawning rate either.

4	

Whatever the reason for yawning, there is no doubt that it is refreshing. According to Ronald Baenninger, another psychologist who is interested in the subject, this feeling is not caused by oxygen coming into the body. The cause, he believes, may lie in the blood: yawning sends an extra supply of blood to the brain. We do not know exactly what the blood does when it reaches the brain, but Baenninger believes it does help to refresh it.

5	

Baenninger believes, therefore, that we yawn in order to make our brains ready for some new action. To test this theory, he asked people to wear bands around their wrists as they went about their normal routines. These bands were sensitive to increased movement by the people wearing them. The bands contained a button which the people were told to press every time they yawned. After collecting data for two weeks, Baenninger found that within 15 minutes of yawning his subjects were normally engaged in some more lively form of activity.

6	

There are indeed plenty of indications from everyday life to suggest that yawning helps the brain to get ready for something big. Olympic athletes yawn before a race, students yawn before an examination, and violinists yawn before a concert. It is not that the athletes, students or violinists are bored; they are simply working to get to a level at which they are well and truly ready for the main event.

7	

'We yawn when there is nothing actually happening but when we do not want to lose our level of readiness,' says Baenninger. Why we yawn before going to bed, though, remains a mystery. Baenninger suggests that it may be that we struggle to stay awake and alert, but sleep simply wins out in the end.

Part 2

You are going to read an extract from a novel. For questions **8-15**, choose the answer (**A**, **B**, **C** or **D**) which you think fits best according to the text.

Mark your answers **on the separate answer sheet**.

On Saturday mornings I worked in the family shop. I started cycling down to the shop with Dad on Saturdays as soon as I was big enough. I thought of it as giving him a hand and so I didn't mind what I did, although it was mostly just fetching and carrying at a run all morning. I managed not to think of it as work and I looked forward to the bar of chocolate my grandmother passed me unsmilingly as I left. I tried not to look at her; I had reason to feel guilty because I'd generally already eaten some dried fruits or a sliver of cheese when no one was looking. As soon as I was fifteen, though, Dad said, 'That's it, our Janet. You're of working age now and you're not coming to work unless your grandmother pays you properly.' He did his best to make his chin look determined. 'I shall speak to her.'

The next Saturday, Gran called me into her little office behind the shop. I always hated going in there. She had an electric heater on full blast, and the windows were always kept tightly closed whatever the weather. 'You're wanting to get paid, I hear,' she said. 'Yes, please,' I replied. It was rather like visiting the headmistress at school, so I was very quiet and respectful. Gran searched through the mess of papers on her crowded desk, sighing and clicking her tongue. Eventually she produced an official-looking leaflet and ran her fingers along the columns of figures. 'How old are you?' 'Fifteen … Gran,' I added for extra politeness, but she looked at me as if I had been cheeky. 'Full-timers at your age get forty pounds for a thirty-five-hour week,' she announced in such a way as to leave no doubt that she wasn't in favour of this. 'No wonder there's no profit in shopkeeping! So, Janet, what's that per hour?' Questions like that always flustered me. Instead of trying to work them out in my head, I would just stand there, unable to think straight. 'I'll get a pencil and paper,' I offered. 'Don't bother,' snapped Gran angrily, 'I'll do it myself. I'll give you a pound an hour; take it or leave it.' 'I'll take it, please.' 'And I expect real work for it, mind. No standing about, and if I catch you eating any of the stock, there'll be trouble. That's theft, and it's a crime.'

From then on, my main job at the shop was filling the shelves. This was dull, but I hardly expected to be trusted with handling the money. Once or twice, however, when Dad was extra busy, I'd tried to help him by serving behind the counter. I hated it. It was very difficult to remember the prices of everything and I was particularly hopeless at using the till. Certain customers made unkind remarks about this, increasing my confusion and the chances of my making a fool of myself.

It was an old-established village shop, going back 150 years at least and it was really behind the times even then. Dad longed to be able to make the shop more attractive to customers, but Gran wouldn't hear of it. I overheard them once arguing about whether to buy a freezer cabinet. 'Our customers want frozen food,' Dad said. 'They see things advertised and if they can't get them from us, they'll go elsewhere.' 'Your father always sold fresh food,' Gran replied. 'People come here for quality, they don't want all that frozen stuff.'

Actually, she gave way in the end over the freezer. Mr Timson, her great rival, installed one in his shop at the other end of the village and customers started making loud comments about how handy it was, being able to get frozen food in the village, and how good Mr Timson's sausages were. That really upset her because she was proud of her sausages and she ungraciously gave Dad the money to buy the freezer. Within a couple of weeks, she was eating frozen food like the rest of us.

8   How did Janet feel when she first started her Saturday morning job?

   A   She enjoyed the work that she was given.
   B   She was pleased to be helping her father.
   C   She worried that she was not doing it well.
   D   She was only really interested in the reward.

9   What do we learn about her grandmother's office in paragraph two?

   A   It needed decorating.
   B   It was untidy.
   C   It had too much furniture in it.
   D   It was dark.

10   'This' (line 18) refers to

   A   shopkeepers' profits.
   B   a thirty-five-hour week.
   C   Janet's request.
   D   the recommended wage.

11   'Flustered' (line 19) means

   A   bored.
   B   angered.
   C   confused.
   D   depressed.

12   Why did Janet's grandmother react angrily to her offer to fetch a pencil and paper?

   A   Janet was unable to answer her question.
   B   Janet had been unwilling to help her.
   C   Janet had made an unhelpful suggestion.
   D   Janet had answered her rudely.

13   What did Janet's father and grandmother disagree about?

   A   how to keep their customers loyal to the shop
   B   the type of advertising needed to attract customers
   C   the type of customers they needed to attract
   D   how to get new customers to come to the shop

14   What eventually persuaded Janet's grandmother to buy a freezer?

   A   She found that she liked frozen food after all.
   B   A new shop opening in the village had one.
   C   It was suggested that her products weren't fresh.
   D   She responded to pressure from her customers.

15   What impression do we get of Janet's feelings towards her grandmother?

   A   She respected her fairness.
   B   She doubted her judgement.
   C   She disliked her manner.
   D   She admired her determination.

Part 3

You are going to read an article written by someone who lives in a house in a valley. Seven sentences have been removed from the article. Choose from the sentences **A-H** the one which fits each gap (**16-21**). There is one extra sentence which you do not need to use. There is an example at the beginning (**0**).

Mark your answers **on the separate answer sheet**.

LIVING IN THE VALLEY

We had been living in our valley for sixteen months when we first realised the dangers that could exist. **0** **H** Until then, we had felt safe and sheltered in our valley.

Soon snow began to fall. Within a day it lay some 15 centimetres deep. **16** But on the neighbouring heights the snow was much deeper and stayed for longer. Up there the wind blasted fiercely. Deep in our valley we felt only sudden gusts of wind; trees swayed but the branches held firm.

And yet we knew that there was reason for us to worry. The snow and wind were certainly inconvenient but they did not really trouble us greatly. **17** It reminded us of what could have occurred if circumstances had been different, if the flow of water from the hills had not, many years before, been controlled, held back by a series of dams.

In a short time the snow started to melt. Day after day, we watched furious clouds pile up high over the hills to the west. Sinister grey clouds extended over the valleys. **18** We had seen enough of the sky; now we began to watch the river, which every day was becoming fuller and wilder.

The snow was gradually washed away as more and more rain streamed from the clouds, but high up in the hills the reservoir was filling and was fast approaching danger level. And then it happened – for the first time in years the reservoir overflowed. **19**

The river seemed maddened as the waters poured almost horizontally down to its lower stretches. Just a couple of metres from our cottage, the stream seemed wild beneath the bridge. **20** [ ] For three days we prayed that it would stay below its wall. Our prayers were answered as the dam held and the waters began to subside.

On many occasions through the centuries before the dam was built, the river had flooded the nearby villages in just such a rage. Now, though, the dam restricts the flow of the river and usually all is well; the great mass of water from the hills, the product of snow and torrential rain, remains behind its barrier with just the occasional overflow. **21** [ ] We can feel our home in the valley is still secure and safe.

A It was the river, the Ryburn, which normally flowed so gently, that threatened us most.

B And yet the immense power of all this water above us prevents us from ever believing ourselves to be completely safe in our home.

C They twisted and turned, rising eastwards and upwards, warning of what was to come.

D It was far deeper than we'd ever seen it so near our home, lunging furiously at its banks.

E We can thus enjoy, rather than fear, the huge clouds that hang over the valley, and can be thrilled by the tremendous power which we know the river possesses.

F It almost completely blocked our lane and made the streamside path slippery and dangerous.

G There in the heights it was like the Niagara Falls, as the water surged over the edge of the dam and poured into the stream below.

H It was the year when the storms came early, before the calendar even hinted at winter, even before November was out.

Part 4

You are going to read a magazine article in which five people talk about their characters. For questions **22-35**, choose from the people (**A-E**). The people may be chosen more than once. When more than one answer is required, these may be given in any order. There is an example at the beginning (**0**).

Mark your answers **on the separate answer sheet**.

Which person or people state(s) the following?

I used to avoid giving my opinions at work.	**0**	E

Taking time off for your professional development can make you feel more self-assured.	**22**	

I never thought I'd be a confident person.	**23**

I'm not influenced by people's opinions of me.	**24**

Everyone gets nervous at times.	**25**	**26**	

Initially, I misunderstood what confidence was.	**27**

I find making notes very supportive in my work.	**28**

A certain event changed the course of my life.	**29**	**30**	

I've worked on having a confident appearance.	**31**

I am realistic about my abilities.	**32**	**33**	

My behaviour helps others relax too.	**34**

Getting things wrong can have a positive result.	**35**

Confident people
What's their secret?

Confident people may look as though they were born that way, but most will tell you that it's a skill they've learned because they had to. Nina Hathway asks five people how they did it.

A   Jenny

When I left school I was very shy and I always thought I'd stay that way. I was about twenty-five when I was asked to help out at my daughter's school. I was sure I wouldn't cope, but I surprised myself by doing well and someone there suggested that I should do a university course.

There was a huge knot in my stomach the day I turned up for my first lecture. But my confidence gradually grew – I became more outgoing. Looking back, working at the school was the turning point in my life that has helped everything else fall into place.

B   Michaela

It all started four years ago when my father became ill and I had to take over the family business. I was so scared, I went over the top and became a bit too aggressive and impatient. I thought that was what confident people were like, but gradually I learned otherwise. To be confident you've got to believe in yourself.

If things get too demanding for me at work, I don't let myself feel guilty if I save a number of tasks until the next day. When I'm confronted with something difficult, I tell myself that I've got nothing to lose. It's fear that makes you lack confidence, so I'm always having quiet chats with myself to put aside those fears!

C   Carol

People think I'm very confident but, in fact, the calmer I look, the more terrified I really am. I've had to develop the ability to look confident because it's the most vital thing in TV. Interviewing people has helped me realise that most – if not all – of us get tense in important situations, and we feel calmer when we speak to someone who's genuinely friendly. The best ever piece of advice came from my mother when I was agonising as a teenager about wearing the right clothes. She simply cried, 'Who's looking at you? Everybody's too busy worrying about how they look.' I've found that's well worth remembering.

I also think you gain confidence by tackling things that scare you. When I took my driving test I was so nervous, but I passed. After that I felt sure that I'd never feel so frightened again, and I never have.

D   Barbara

My confidence comes naturally from really enjoying the work I do, but it's something that I've built up over the years. If you just get on with it and learn from any mistakes you make, you're more confident the next time round. I work hard and I'm popular in the restaurant, but it's probable that one out of ten people doesn't like me. I don't let that affect me. You've got to like yourself for what you are, not try to be what others expect.

My company runs a lot of training courses, and going on those has built up my self-esteem. The company also encourages employees to set manageable targets. It helps no end if you can see you're achieving something tangible, rather than reaching for the stars all at once, and ending up with nothing but air!

E   Elaine

After I left college I worked for years as a secretary and would sit in meetings, not always agreeing with what was being said, but too scared to speak up. Eventually, I summoned up the confidence to start making my point. Even so, when I first worked in politics, I'd never spoken in public before and always used to shake like a leaf. I would say to myself, 'Don't be so silly. People do this every day of their lives, so there's no reason why you can't.' I also found it helpful to jot a few things down to refer to – rather like having a comfort blanket!

I don't think there is anyone who isn't a little shaky when it comes to talking publicly. The real secret of confidence lies in telling yourself over and over again, 'Nothing is impossible.'

PAPER 2 WRITING (1 hour 30 minutes)

Part 1

You **must** answer this question.

1   Your English friend, Peter, has written to you asking you to help him organise a special surprise birthday party for his sister, Anna.

Read Peter's letter and the notes you have made. Then, using all the information, write to Peter answering his questions **and** explaining how you think the party could be made special.

We must make sure that Anna has no idea we're planning such a great surprise! I'm not sure how many people to invite but anyway our house is certainly too small. Do you think we should book the Majestic Hotel in town for the evening?

Sounds good – but expensive?

Anna loves music so we'll have a live band after the meal. What sort of food would be best? I've spent ages thinking about what we could all buy her as a present and I thought a watch would be a good idea. What do you think?

A birthday cake and …

No, because …

Anna enjoys travelling so …

Can you come the day before to help with the preparations? There's a lot to think about so, as you can see, I really need your help! Also can you suggest something else that will make this party really special?

Sorry – busy that day

Best wishes

Peter

Yes. How about …

Write a **letter** of between **120** and **180** words in an appropriate style on the opposite page. Do not write any postal addresses.

Question 1

Part 2

Write an answer to **one** of the questions 2-5 in this part. Write your answer in **120-180** words in an appropriate style on the opposite page. Put the question number in the box.

2   You have been doing a class project on transport. Your teacher has now asked you to write a composition about the following statement:

There is no future for public transport, because travelling by car is so much more convenient.

Write your **composition**.

3   You see this advertisement for a job in the USA.

USA SUMMER CAMPS

People of all ages needed to work in summer camps all over the USA.

If you can speak English and you are cheerful, energetic and hardworking, you are the right person for us. Food and accommodation are provided. You just pay the air fare.

You will: – look after children aged 8–12
              – help organise sports and evening activities
              – work in the kitchens

Write telling us about yourself and why you think you would be a suitable person for the job.

Write your **letter of application**. Do not write any postal addresses.

4   An international student magazine is running a short story competition which you have decided to enter. The story must **end** with the following words:

Michael closed the door and knew at that moment he had made a mistake.

Write your **story**.

5   Answer **one** of the following two questions based on your reading of **one** of these set books. Write (**a**) or (**b**) as well as the number **5** in the question box, and the **title** of the book next to the box. Your answer **must** be about one of the books below.

Best Detective Stories of Agatha Christie – Longman Fiction
A Tale of Two Cities – Charles Dickens
Animal Farm – George Orwell
Wuthering Heights – Emily Brontë
More Tales from Shakespeare – Charles and Mary Lamb

Either (a)   'How important is the title of a book or short story?' Your teacher has asked you to write a **composition** discussing this question and explaining why the writer of the book or one of the short stories you have read chose that particular title.

Or   (b)   The English book club you belong to is producing a list of books in English which it can recommend to members. The Club Secretary has asked you to write a **report** on the book or short stories you have read, saying whether this book would be suitable to include on the list and explaining why.

Question [   ]

....
....
....
....
....
....
....
....
....
....
....
....
....
....
....
....
....
....
....
....
....
....
....
....
....
....
....
....
....

PAPER 3   USE OF ENGLISH (1 hour 15 minutes)

Part 1

For questions **1-15**, read the text below and decide which answer (**A**, **B**, **C** or **D**) best fits each space. There is an example at the beginning (**0**).

Mark your answers **on the separate answer sheet**.

Example:

0   A   celebrates   **B**   shows   **C**   honours   **D**   demonstrates

0	A	B	C	D
	—	⸱	⸱	⸱

EVERYONE'S AN ARTIST

Every year, the village of Pettineo **(0)** ..... its unique arts festival. For a few days each summer, artists from all over Europe **(1)** ..... at this village near the north coast of Sicily to **(2)** ..... the creative atmosphere. During their stay, the artists get **(3)** ..... with the local people to paint a one-kilometre long picture that runs the **(4)** ..... of the high street. **(5)** ..... the painting is done, each visiting artist joins a local family for a big lunch and, **(6)** ..... the meal, the family receives the **(7)** ..... of the painting that the artist has painted. As a result, **(8)** ..... few villagers are rich, almost every home has at least one painting by a well-known European artist. Visitors to the village are eagerly **(9)** ..... into homes to see these paintings.

The festival was the **(10)** ..... of Antonio Presti, a local businessman who **(11)** ..... it up four years ago. Since then, Pettineo has **(12)** ..... a sort of domestic art museum in **(13)** ..... any visitor can ring a doorbell, go into a house and **(14)** ..... a painting. In addition to this exhibition of paintings in people's homes, for those who have time to spare, there is an opportunity to **(15)** ..... through the display of huge sculptures in the village square.

1	**A** group	**B** crowd	**C** gather	**D** combine
2	**A** amuse	**B** enjoy	**C** entertain	**D** delight
3	**A** linked	**B** jointly	**C** combined	**D** together
4	**A** size	**B** measure	**C** length	**D** area
5	**A** Just	**B** Once	**C** Soon	**D** Only
6	**A** in addition to	**B** in place of	**C** in common with	**D** in exchange for
7	**A** partition	**B** section	**C** division	**D** region
8	**A** though	**B** despite	**C** since	**D** even
9	**A** persuaded	**B** invited	**C** requested	**D** attracted
10	**A** image	**B** purpose	**C** thought	**D** idea
11	**A** set	**B** put	**C** got	**D** had
12	**A** become	**B** advanced	**C** grown	**D** increased
13	**A** what	**B** where	**C** whom	**D** which
14	**A** wonder	**B** stare	**C** admire	**D** delight
15	**A** move	**B** step	**C** wander	**D** march

Part 2

For questions **16-30**, read the text below and think of the word which best fits each space. Use only **one** word in each space. There is an example at the beginning (**0**).
Write your answers **on the separate answer sheet**.

Example: | **0** | *with* |

PROBLEMS FOR ACTORS

Many actors do not like working (**0**) ...*with*... children or animals. This is probably (**16**) .... they are afraid that the audience may become (**17**) .... interested in the children and animals than in them.

Actors can have problems (**18**) .... a different kind when they (**19**) .... required to eat or drink on stage. If they have (**20**) .... much food in their mouths, the words they say may not (**21**) .... clear, and they may even end up coughing and choking.

Other problems can occur with food (**22**) .... films are being made. In a recent film, during (**23**) .... a family was waiting to have a meal, one of the actors entered with a large roast chicken on a tray and then (**24**) .... to begin to cut some meat from it while he was speaking. By mistake, the actor cut off a whole leg of the chicken and then completely forgot (**25**) .... his next words were. It was necessary to film the scene (**26**) .... This (**27**) .... not really have mattered (**28**) .... there had been another roast chicken in the studio, but there was not. At (**29**) ...., nobody knew what to do, but eventually the problem was solved (**30**) .... putting a nail in the leg and attaching it back onto the chicken.

Part 3

For questions **31-40**, complete the second sentence so that it has a similar meaning to the first sentence, using the word given. **Do not change the word given**. You must use between **two** and **five** words, including the word given.

Here is an example (**0**).

Example:

0   You must do exactly what the manager tells you.

   carry

   You must .... instructions exactly.

The gap can be filled by the words 'carry out the manager's' so you write:

0	*carry out the manager's*

Write **only the missing words** on the separate answer sheet.

---

31   John is interested in knowing more about astronomy.

   like

   John .... more about astronomy.

32   Because of the parade, we weren't allowed to park in the High Street.

   let

   Because of the parade, the police wouldn't ....
   in the High Street.

33   'Did you see that film on television on Saturday?' Susan asked me.

   seen

   Susan wanted to know .... that film on
   television on Saturday.

34   'I'm afraid these jeans have a hole in them.'

   there

   'I'm afraid that .... these jeans.'

35 They cancelled the match because of the bad weather.

called

The match .... because of the bad weather.

36 Dan never takes any notice of my advice.

attention

Dan never .... my advice.

37 'Can I borrow your bicycle, Sarah?' asked Frank.

lend

Frank asked Sarah .... her bicycle.

38 Maybe Peter forgot that we changed the time of the meeting.

might

Peter .... that we changed the time of the meeting.

39 She checks the company accounts very efficiently.

efficient

She's very .... the company accounts.

40 All the children enjoy themselves at this summer camp.

fun

Every .... at this summer camp.

Part 4

For questions **41-55**, read the text below and look carefully at each line. Some of the lines are correct, and some have a word which should not be there.

If a line is correct, put a tick (✓) by the number **on the separate answer sheet**. If a line has a word which should **not** be there, write the word **on the separate answer sheet**. There are two examples at the beginning (**0** and **00**).

Examples:

0	✓
00	*of*

A LETTER OF COMPLAINT

0	I am writing to complain about our recent holiday, which involved
00	several last-minute changes to the arrangements, despite of the fact
41	that we had made our booking for several months in advance.
42	The journey to the coast took four hours longer than your
43	brochure suggested. The coach which took us was far too much old
44	and the last part of the journey was terrifying, as if the driver tried to
45	make up for the time we had lost. However, this was nothing
46	compared with our own horror when we arrived at the hotel. Your
47	advertisement promised to us large rooms with colour television. In fact,
48	our bedroom was hardly that big enough to lie down in and the only
49	television was in the lounge. We did not go downstairs for eat an evening
50	meal, but decided instead to go to the bed straightaway.
51	It was quite clear that we could not enjoy our holiday in this hotel.
52	Your representative was no help at all, so we had to find
53	somewhere else to stay at for the rest of the week ourselves.
54	I expect you to return the money we paid for this trip, which it totally
55	failed to live up to the claims made in your brochure.

Part 5

For questions **56-65**, read the text below. Use the word given in capitals at the end of each line to form a word that fits in the space in the same line. There is an example at the beginning (**0**). Write your answers **on the separate answer sheet**.

Example:
0	*growth*

AIRPORTS

With the (**0**) .*growth*. in air travel, airports have become symbols of	**GROW**
international importance, and are (**56**) ..... designed by well-known	**FREQUENT**
architects. Airports have (**57**) ..... facilities nowadays.	**IMPRESS**
There are (**58**) ..... departure lounges, where passengers wait	**COMFORT**
before boarding their (**59**) ..... , restaurants, shopping areas and	**FLY**
banks. Good road and rail (**60**) ..... with nearby towns and cities are also	**COMMUNICATE**
essential.	
However, it is becoming (**61**) ..... difficult to find land on	**INCREASE**
which to build airports, as aircraft, despite (**62**) ..... in	**IMPROVE**
engine design, are (**63**) ..... , and need a considerable amount of	**NOISE**
space in which to land and take off. (**64**) ..... residential areas	**CROWD**
need to be avoided, so, (**65**) ..... , suitable land might be an	**FORTUNATE**
inconvenient distance away from the city.	

PAPER 4   LISTENING (approximately 40 minutes)

Part 1

You will hear people talking in eight different situations. For questions **1-8**, choose the best answer (**A**, **B** or **C**).

1   You overhear two people talking in a restaurant.
    Where has the woman just come from?

    A   a supermarket

    B   a hospital

    C   a football match

2   You hear a man talking about a mobile phone he has bought.
    What most attracted him to this phone?

    A   its size

    B   its reliability

    C   its price

3   You hear a man talking on the phone about buying a house.
    What is the purpose of his call?

    A   to apologise

    B   to complain

    C   to obtain information

4   You hear a teenage girl talking about her hobby.
    What is she talking about?

    A   a computer game

    B   a musical instrument

    C   a piece of sports equipment

5 On the news, you hear a story about a cat.
   Where was the cat found?

   A in a train carriage

   B on the railway lines

   C on a station platform

6 You hear a woman talking about how she gets ideas for her work.
   Who is the woman?

   A a novelist

   B an artist

   C a film-maker

7 You hear two people talking.
   How does the woman feel?

   A surprised

   B satisfied

   C relieved

8 You turn on the radio and hear a man speaking.
   What are you listening to?

   A a history programme

   B a science-fiction story

   C an advertisement

Part 2

You will hear a radio interview with a woman who is organising a training weekend for
people interested in the theatre. For questions **9-18**, complete the notes.

TRAINING WEEKEND

WHEN: beginning of [_____ **9**]

CONTENT: Saturday – two groups run by professionals

     subjects: [_____ **10**] or directing

     Sunday – two groups

     subjects: make-up or press and [_____ **11**]

WHERE: mostly [_____ **12**] (at the theatre)

COST: whole weekend course (if booked):

[_____ **13**] (includes lunches)

**COURSE
LEADERS:** have training as [_____ **14**]

**MAIN
AGE GROUP:** [_____ **15**]

**LAST YEAR'S
TRAINING DAY:** concentrated on [_____ **16**]

HOW TO APPLY: name of person to phone: Claire [_____ **17**]

official position of person:

[_____ **18**] (at the theatre)

Part 3

You will hear five different students who are studying away from home. They are talking about their accommodation. For questions **19-23**, choose from the list (**A-F**) what each speaker says about their accommodation. Use the letters only once. There is one extra letter which you do not need to use.

A   I made a mistake there at first.

Speaker 1 | 19

B   I was able to settle into a new area.

Speaker 2 | 20

C   I had no choice in the matter.

Speaker 3 | 21

D   I have recommended it to others.

Speaker 4 | 22

E   There are more benefits than disadvantages.

Speaker 5 | 23

F   I would prefer to have more freedom.

Part 4

You will hear part of a radio interview in which Tina White, a magazine editor, talks about her life and work. For questions **24-30**, choose the best answer (**A**, **B** or **C**).

24   In her first column, Tina chose to write about people who

    A   were very well known.

    B   had interesting ideas.

    C   lived in luxury.

24

25   She took up journalism because of

    A   her family connections.

    B   her father's support.

    C   her love for books.

25

26   Under her management, the magazine *Female Focus*

    A   reduced its losses.

    B   changed its image.

    C   made a profit.

26

27   She believes people are more likely to read an article if

    A   it has a good beginning.

    B   its content is challenging.

    C   it is mentioned on the cover.

27

28   When she started her present job five years ago, she

    A   organised her ideal team.

    B   had more time to read everything.

    C   lacked confidence in her staff.

28

29   Tina says that she would be worried if she

    A   was criticised by the public.

    B   lost the respect of colleagues.

    C   lost her job.

29

30   In the future, she would like to

    A   be a book editor.

    B   produce a film.

    C   write fiction.

30

PAPER 5   SPEAKING (14 minutes)

You take the Speaking test with another candidate, referred to here as your partner. There are two examiners. One will speak to you and your partner and the other will be listening. Both examiners will award marks.

Part 1 (3 minutes)

The examiner asks you and your partner questions about yourselves. You may be asked about things like 'your home town', 'your interests', 'your career plans', etc.

Part 2 (4 minutes)

The examiner gives you two photographs and asks you to talk about them for one minute. The examiner then asks your partner a question about your photographs and your partner responds briefly.

Then the examiner gives your partner two different photographs. Your partner talks about these photographs for one minute. This time the examiner asks you a question about your partner's photographs and you respond briefly.

Part 3 (approximately 3 minutes)

The examiner asks you and your partner to talk together. You may be asked to solve a problem or try to come to a decision about something. For example, you might be asked to decide the best way to use some rooms in a language school. The examiner gives you a picture to help you but does not join in the conversation.

Part 4 (approximately 4 minutes)

The examiner joins in the conversation. You all talk together in a more general way about what has been said in Part 3. The examiner asks you questions but you and your partner are also expected to develop the conversation.

Test 3

PAPER 1   READING (1 hour 15 minutes)

Part 1

You are going to read a magazine article about human behaviour. Choose from the list **A-I** the sentence which best summarises each part (**1-7**) of the article. There is one extra sentence which you do not need to use. There is an example at the beginning (**0**).

Mark your answers **on the separate answer sheet**.

A   People are very keen to be skilful at misleading others.

B   People are sometimes unable to hide the fact that they are being dishonest.

C   Instinct plays an important part in our development.

D   People seldom realise that their faces are showing that they are being dishonest.

E   It is not easy for anyone to detect dishonesty.

F   People form judgements about other people just by looking at their faces.

G   Being good at fooling others may be a sign of high intelligence.

H   The way that feelings are shown is common to a great many people.

I   It is strange that people often do not realise when others are being dishonest with them.

Facing the truth

Our facial expressions provide a clear map of our emotions.
But some people cannot read the signposts ...

0 | I

Our brains have been processing sophisticated information via our senses for millions of years. So why is it we are still vulnerable to lies? Why aren't we better at discovering the deception of others?

1

The language of the face is emotion. Almost our first sight as a new-born baby is our mother's face smiling at us. Not only are we immediately programmed to respond to faces, but right away we can also signal surprise, pleasure and distress. The constant visual dialogue, as parent and child mirror expressions back and forth, is vital for the young brain. It is how we build a sense of other minds – we feel happy when we smile, so someone else smiling must be feeling the same.

2

Not only is the emotional language of the face vital to normal functioning, it also seems to be almost universal, says Paul Ekman, a leading researcher in the subject. 'Wherever you are, anger, happiness, fear, disgust, sadness and surprise look the same.'

3

But we make all sorts of false assumptions about faces. Attractive people, for instance, may get the benefit of the doubt. We sometimes assume they are kinder, cleverer and more honest than those with less regular features. Then we have other unconscious biases about certain kinds of face. In a woman, certain facial features may be thought attractive, but the same features may mark a man out as weak.

4

These are just some of the ways we fool ourselves. So why aren't we better at detecting liars? Because for millions of years humans have been in a battle with each other to develop better techniques for deception. We are highly social animals and our survival depends not only on cooperating with others but also on getting an advantage when we can. In fact, one theory claims that the ability to cheat, to make others in the group think an expression means friendship rather than anger, is one of the most important factors driving human development.

5

Some believe it is also related to how bright we are. 'We have found a strong relationship between the ability to deceive and brain power,' says Leda Cosmides, a psychologist at the University of California. 'The more developed people's minds are, the better they are at concealing their intentions and manipulating others for their own ends.'

6

Humans are simply the biggest liars on the planet and we start lying convincingly from a very early age. Studies show that even people who deal with deception professionally, such as judges and policemen, score only about 50% – the same as the rest of us – when asked to rate people as to whether they are telling the truth or not on videotape.

7

Our voices, however, can betray our intention. Dr Richard Williams of Hereford University has found that when people are blindfolded, they can spot the difference between someone telling the truth and a lie about 75% of the time. 'Most people, when they are lying, are rarely aware that they've started to speak more softly or more slowly,' he says.

Part 2

You are going to read an article about a man who makes works of art out of sea shells. For questions **8-15**, choose the answer (**A**, **B**, **C** or **D**) which you think fits best according to the text.

Mark your answers **on the separate answer sheet**.

THE SHELL ARTIST

At the age of 83 Peter Cooke has become a master of his art.

There are still many things that Peter Cooke would like to try his hand at – paper-making and feather-work are on his list. For the moment though, he will stick to the skill that he has been delighted to perfect over the past ten years: making delicate and unusual objects out of shells.

'Tell me if I am boring you,' he says, as he leads me round his apartment showing me his work. There is a fine line between being a bore and being an enthusiast, but Cooke need not worry: he fits into the latter category, helped both by his charm and by the beauty of the things he makes.

He points to a pair of shell-covered ornaments above a fireplace. 'I shan't be at all bothered if people don't buy them because I have got so used to them, and to me they're adorable. I never meant to sell my work commercially. Some friends came to see me about five years ago and said, "You must have an exhibition – people ought to see these. We'll talk to a man who owns an art gallery".' The result was an exhibition in London, at which 70 per cent of the objects were sold. His second exhibition opened at the gallery yesterday. Considering the enormous prices the pieces command – around £2,000 for the ornaments – an empty space above the
25 fireplace would seem a small sacrifice for Cooke to make.

There are 86 pieces in the exhibition, with prices starting at £225 for a shell-flower in a crystal vase. Cooke insists that he has nothing to do with the prices and is cheerily open about their level: he claims there is nobody else in the world who produces work like his, and, as the gallery-owner told him, 'Well, you're going to stop one day and everybody will want your pieces because there won't be any more.'

'I do wish, though,' says Cooke, 'that I'd taken this up a lot earlier, because then I would have been able to produce really wonderful things – at least the potential would have been there. Although the ideas are still there and I'm doing the best I can now, I'm more limited physically than I was when I started.' Still, the work that he has managed to produce is a long way from the common shell constructions that can be found in seaside shops. 'I have a miniature mind,' he says, and this has resulted in boxes covered in thousands of tiny shells, little shaded pictures made from shells and baskets of astonishingly realistic flowers.

Cooke has created his own method and uses materials as and when he finds them. He uses the cardboard sent back with laundered shirts for his flower bases, a nameless glue bought in bulk from a sail-maker ('If it runs out, I don't know what I will do!') and washing-up liquid to wash the shells. 'I have an idea of what I want to do, and it just does itself,' he says of his working method, yet the attention to detail, colour gradations and symmetry he achieves look far from accidental.

Cooke's quest for beautiful, and especially tiny, shells has taken him further than his Norfolk shore: to France, Thailand, Mexico, South Africa and the Philippines, to name but a few of the beaches where he has lain on his stomach and looked for beauties to bring home. He is insistent that he only collects dead shells and defends himself against people who write him letters accusing him of stripping the world's beaches. 'When I am collecting shells, I hear people's great fat feet crunching them up far faster than I can collect them; and the ones that are left, the sea breaks up. I would not dream of collecting shells with living creatures in them or diving for them, but once their occupants have left, why should I not collect them?' If one bases this argument on the amount of luggage that can be carried home by one man, the sum beauty of whose work is often greater than its natural parts, it becomes very convincing indeed. 72

8   What does the reader learn about Peter Cooke in the first paragraph?

  A   He has produced hand-made objects in different materials.

  B   He was praised for his shell objects many years ago.

  C   He hopes to work with other materials in the future.

  D   He has written about his love of making shell objects.

9   When looking round his apartment, the writer

  A   is attracted by Cooke's personality.

  B   senses that Cooke wants his products to be admired.

  C   realises he finds Cooke's work boring.

  D   feels uncertain about giving Cooke his opinion.

10   The 'small sacrifice' in line 25 refers to

  A   the loss of Cooke's ornaments.

  B   the display of Cooke's ornaments.

  C   the cost of keeping Cooke's ornaments.

  D   the space required to store Cooke's ornaments.

11   When the writer enquires about the cost of his shell objects, Cooke

  A   cleverly changes the subject.

  B   defends the prices charged for his work.

  C   says he has no idea why the level is so high.

  D   notes that his work will not always be so popular.

12   What does Cooke regret about his work?

  A   He is not as famous as he should have been.

  B   He makes less money than he should make.

  C   He is less imaginative than he used to be.

  D   He is not as skilful as he used to be.

13   When talking about the artist's working method, the writer suspects that Cooke

  A   accepts that he sometimes makes mistakes.

  B   is unaware of the unique quality his work has.

  C   underrates his creative contribution.

  D   undervalues the materials that he uses.

14   What does the reader learn about Cooke's shell-collecting activities?

  A   Not everyone approves of what he does.

  B   Other methods might make his work easier.

  C   Other tourists get in the way of his collecting.

  D   Not all shells are the right size and shape for his work.

15   What does 'it' in line 72 refer to?

  A   Cooke's luggage

  B   Cooke's argument

  C   the beauty of Cooke's work

  D   the reason for Cooke's trips

Part 3

You are going to read a magazine article about a new hotel. Eight sentences have been removed from the article. Choose from the sentences **A-I** the one which fits each gap (**16-22**). There is one extra sentence which you do not need to use. There is an example at the beginning (**0**).

Mark your answers **on the separate answer sheet**.

Five-star luxury meets up-to-date technology

The five-star Merrion Hotel, which has just opened, is the result of considerable research into customer requirements and nearly two years' work converting four large, eighteenth-century houses in Dublin. **0** **I** This has been done for the benefit of staff and guests alike.

At the Merrion, General Manager Peter MacCann expects his staff to know the guests by name. **16** It can deal with return clients in the extra-special way that is appropriate to a five-star hotel.

Though the system cost £250,000 to install, it will pay for itself over time, according to MacCann. **17** For example, a guest who requests certain music CDs during a first stay will find those same CDs ready for him on a return visit. This is thanks to the guest-history facility which allows staff to key in any number of preferences.

Hotel guests the world over frequently complain about room temperature. **18** Guests have the opportunity to change the temperature themselves within three degrees either side of the normal 18°C but, in addition, each individual room can be adjusted by any amount between 14°C and 25°C at the front desk.

19 This is particularly true for the business user, and MacCann estimates that up to sixty-five per cent of his business will come from this part of the market. To provide the best service for such needs, the hotel has taken the traditional business centre and put it into individual bedrooms. Each one has three phones, two phone lines, a fax machine that doubles as a photocopier and printer, and a video-conferencing facility.

Technology changes so quickly these days that the hotel has had to try to forecast possible improvements. **20** The televisions are rented rather than bought, so that they can be replaced with more up-to-date models at any time. Video recorders can also be upgraded when necessary.

Despite the presence of all this very up-to-the-minute equipment in the rooms, MacCann says they have tried hard not to make guests feel threatened by the technology. **21** There are, of course, a swimming pool and gym, six conference rooms, two bars and two restaurants, and a beautiful garden at the heart of it all.

As at all luxury hotels, the food that is offered to guests must be excellent. Chef Patrick Guilbaud's Dublin restaurant already had two Michelin stars when he agreed to move his restaurant business to the Merrion. **22** He has been able to design a new kitchen and take it into the modern age. There are better parking facilities than at the previous address, too. From the hotel's side, they are able to offer a popular and successful place to eat, with no financial risks attached.

Aided by technology and a highly capable staff, the Merrion looks likely to succeed.

A   For guests, though, it is the other technology offered in their rooms which is most likely to find favour.

B   Being part of the hotel site has huge benefits, both for him and the hotel itself.

C   Extra cables have been laid to handle whatever scientific advances may occur.

D   He expects fifty per cent of the rooms to be occupied in the hotel's first year.

E   Another hi-tech system controls this essential area of comfort.

F   However, for details of his guests' preferences, he relies on the hotel's computer system.

G   The one hundred and forty-five bedrooms, large and well-furnished, are both comfortable and welcoming.

H   He praises its efficiency and talks enthusiastically of the facilities it offers.

I   Creating a new hotel in this way has allowed the latest technology to be installed.

Part 4

You are going to read a magazine article about members of a part-time drama club called The Globe Players. For questions **23-35**, choose from the people (**A-F**). The people may be chosen more than once. When more than one answer is required, these may be given in any order. There is an example at the beginning (**0**).

Mark your answers **on the separate answer sheet**.

Which person or people

mentions joining because of loneliness?	**0**	A
had some theatre experience before joining The Globe Players?	**23**	
has a high opinion of The Globe Players?	**24**	
believes the other members are like them in character?	**25**	
has mixed feelings about finishing a show?	**26**	
have difficulty finding suitable roles?	**27**	**28**
enjoys being with people who have different ideas?	**29**	
thinks that acting is out of character for them?	**30**	
mentions the publicity they sometimes receive?	**31**	
joined to keep busy?	**32**	
talks about the complications of putting on a play?	**33**	
feel that not everyone approves of them acting?	**34**	**35**

The Globe Players

A Christina Howard

When I moved to this area the children were quite little, and I wondered how I was ever going to meet people. Then I met Susanna Dickster, who was the organiser of The Globe Players, and she said, 'Do you want to join?' And I said, 'Well, yes, all right.' They appeared to be incredibly extrovert people, which I suppose I am by nature too. For three years I was the theatre manager. I think I make a better manager than an actress, but I did have a dream role in a play the year before last.

B Eric Plumber

I do about one play a year, just out of interest. But I'm a quiet sort of chap, not one of the world's extroverts, and yet here I am in an extrovert field, doing theatrical activities. There is a sort of magic to the theatre. There's a sense of togetherness with the rest of the actors in the cast. When a play is over, on the last night, there's a combination of anticlimax and relief. It's rather nice to think you will be able to do all the things that you weren't able to do when the play was on. But there's also a sense of loss, so you look forward to the next play.

C Laura Goldcrest

I have done some stage management for productions at my school and when I saw the play The Globe Players were going to do next, I thought I'd try for it. Usually there are not a lot of parts for people my age, so when there was this opportunity, I went along and auditioned. It went all right, and I got the part. Lots of my friends just hang around with people of their own age, but there are people at The Globe Players who are quite old, and I get talking to them about all sorts of things. It's amazing how our views differ, but we have lovely conversations.

D Clare MacDonald

When I was at school, I used to think I'd rather like to go on stage. But then other things came along. One job I did was as a stewardess for an airline. That's like giving a performance. I left the airline and joined The Globe Players. My husband will always come to performances, but he does tend to moan a bit because he feels it takes up too much time. As a club I feel we are very professional. I do about one play a year, which is quite enough. Obviously, there are fewer parts as you get older, particularly for women: one can no longer play Juliet or other young parts, which I feel sad about.

E Robin Wilson

I work behind the scenes with The Globe Players because it's always a challenge. For instance, the last play I did needed a full-sized, working swimming pool. Well, most amateur theatres have a bucket of water in the wings. But our director said, 'I want a real swimming pool on that set. Go away and do it.' It was a real challenge for me. However, we did it. We got more reviews than we usually do because, of course, it was something different. And quite a lot of amateur societies came to see if they could do it – and a lot of them decided they couldn't.

F Mike James

I was a science teacher and took early retirement from my college. After twenty-four years it was a bit hard and I got rather bored. During that time it was good to have the drama group. It takes your mind off things; you can't act and worry about something else. But it's very disruptive to a family – my wife will tell you that. Teaching in a way is like being on stage. When you go into a class you may not be feeling very well, you are not necessarily very keen on the subject you are teaching – the whole thing adds up to a no-no. But you go in, you are enthusiastic and you try to generate interest, and it's an act.

PAPER 2   WRITING (1 hour 30 minutes)

Part 1

You **must** answer this question.

1   You are studying in Britain and you have recently received a letter from an English friend who is interested in arranging a day trip for a group of students.

Read the extract from your friend's letter and the advertisement for a boat trip, on which you have made some notes. Then, using all your notes, write a letter to your friend giving the information requested and saying whether you would recommend the trip.

> *The students in my class are really interested in going on a day trip. I know you went on a boat trip with your English class recently. Could you tell me what it was like and whether you'd recommend it?*

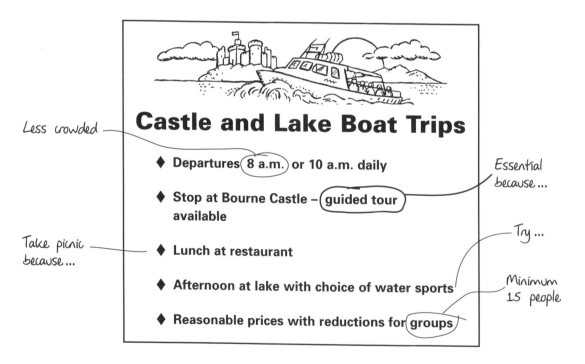

Less crowded

Castle and Lake Boat Trips

♦ Departures 8 a.m. or 10 a.m. daily

Essential because...

♦ Stop at Bourne Castle – guided tour available

Take picnic because...

♦ Lunch at restaurant

Try ...

♦ Afternoon at lake with choice of water sports

Minimum 15 people

♦ Reasonable prices with reductions for groups

Write a **letter** of between **120** and **180** words in an appropriate style on the opposite page. Do not write any postal addresses.

Question 1

Part 2

Write an answer to **one** of the questions **2-5** in this part. Write your answer in **120-180** words in an appropriate style on the opposite page. Put the question number in the box.

2   An English language club is starting in your area. The organisers of the club have asked you to write a report giving your suggestions about:

• how often the club should meet
• what type of activities it should organise
• how the club could be advertised

Write your **report**.

3   You have decided to enter a short story competition in an international magazine. The competition rules say that the story must **begin** with the following words:

It was three o'clock in the morning when the phone rang.

Write your **story**.

4   You have seen this announcement in *Leisure and Entertainment* magazine.

Could you live without television for a week?

Write and tell us what difference this would make to your life.

We will publish the best article.

Write your **article**.

5   Answer **one** of the following two questions based on your reading of **one** of these set books. Write (**a**) or (**b**) as well as the number **5** in the question box, and the **title** of the book next to the box. Your answer **must** be about one of the books below.

Best Detective Stories of Agatha Christie – Longman Fiction
A Tale of Two Cities – Charles Dickens
Animal Farm – George Orwell
Wuthering Heights – Emily Brontë
More Tales from Shakespeare – Charles and Mary Lamb

Either   (**a**)   'Did anything in the book or short story you have read disappoint you?' Write a **composition**, answering this question with reference to the book or one of the short stories you have read.

Or   (**b**)   'For a book to be successful, the author has to show the importance of the relationships between characters.' Is this true of the book or one of the short stories you have read? Write a **composition**, explaining your views.

Question [ ]

....
....
....
....
....
....
....
....
....
....
....
....
....
....
....
....
....
....
....
....
....
....
....
....
....
....
....
....
....
....
....

PAPER 3   USE OF ENGLISH (1 hour 15 minutes)

Part 1

For questions **1-15**, read the text below and decide which answer (**A, B, C** or **D**) best fits each space. There is an example at the beginning (**0**).

Mark your answers **on the separate answer sheet**.

Example:

| **0** | **A** speed | **B** pace | **C** rate | **D** rhythm |

0	**A**	**B**	**C**	**D**
	—	—	—	—

THE NEED FOR BIGGER PLANES

The big issue for plane-makers planning for the future is size, not (**0**) ..... . With the skies already full of air traffic, and with worse to (**1**) ..... , the important questions for the designers are how many passengers they can (**2**) ..... into the new super-planes and who will be (**3**) ..... to build them first.

(**4**) ..... yourself ten years from now in a packed airport departure lounge. Eight hundred passengers are waiting with you for their first flight on one of a remarkable range of super-planes, and the check-in time (**5**) ..... have been as much as four hours before take-off to (**6**) ..... for the extra people. Impossible? Far from it. Designs for these planes are already (**7**) ..... on computer at the world's top aircraft manufacturers, waiting to be turned (**8**) ..... reality.

The airlines badly need the new jets to (**9**) ..... with future increases in passenger (**10**) ..... . A billion passengers a year are currently carried by air, but that figure is (**11**) ..... to double by the year 2010. The only practical (**12**) ..... of avoiding making the skies even busier is to build much bigger planes. The (**13**) ..... to build the new jets is the hottest contest in the airliner business. Manufacturers are working (**14**) ..... with the major airlines to produce designs that will please airlines and passengers (**15**) ..... .

1 **A** go   **B** happen   **C** come   **D** arrive

2 **A** contain   **B** fit   **C** hold   **D** sit

3 **A** possible   **B** able   **C** proper   **D** capable

4 **A** Consider   **B** Suppose   **C** Imagine   **D** Regard

5 **A** can   **B** need   **C** ought   **D** may

6 **A** watch   **B** allow   **C** look   **D** permit

7 **A** supplied   **B** given   **C** stored   **D** carried

8 **A** as   **B** by   **C** into   **D** for

9 **A** deal   **B** treat   **C** manage   **D** succeed

10 **A** amounts   **B** sums   **C** quantities   **D** numbers

11 **A** expected   **B** thought   **C** known   **D** hoped

12 **A** scheme   **B** process   **C** way   **D** plan

13 **A** game   **B** sport   **C** match   **D** race

14 **A** tightly   **B** strongly   **C** closely   **D** firmly

15 **A** equal   **B** alike   **C** similar   **D** same

Part 2

For questions **16-30**, read the text below and think of the word which best fits each space. Use only **one** word in each space. There is an example at the beginning (**0**). Write your answers **on the separate answer sheet**.

Example: | **0** | *his* |

CHARLES DICKENS' CHILDHOOD EXPERIENCES

Charles Dickens was one of the greatest nineteenth-century English novelists. At the time of (**0**) ...*his*.... death in 1870 he was a wealthy man, in contrast to the poverty of his early days. His parents (**16**) .... their best to look after him but were always in difficulties (**17**) .... money. Eventually, his father owed (**18**) .... a large amount of money that he was sent to prison for three months.

Two days after his twelfth birthday, Dickens was taken away from school by his parents and made (**19**) .... work in a factory in London to increase the family income. Factories could be dangerous places in (**20**) .... days and some employers were cruel. Charles was not (**21**) .... extremely unhappy, but also ashamed of working there, and he (**22**) .... never forget that period of his life. Years later, (**23**) .... his novel 'Oliver Twist', Dickens described his own childhood experiences. Oliver Twist was one of his most famous characters and he too suffered (**24**) .... a child worker. Dickens' novels showed how shocking working and living conditions (**25**) .... Working in the factory affected him so deeply that he found (**26**) .... much too painful to speak about in later life. His own wife and children knew (**27**) .... at all about the unhappiness of his childhood while Dickens was still alive, (**28**) .... shortly after his death a biography was published in (**29**) .... Dickens' terrible childhood experiences in the factory were revealed (**30**) .... the first time.

Part 3

For questions **31-40**, complete the second sentence so that it has a similar meaning to the first sentence, using the word given. **Do not change the word given**. You must use between **two** and **five** words, including the word given.

Here is an example (**0**).

Example:

0   You must do exactly what the manager tells you.

carry

You must .... instructions exactly.

The gap can be filled by the words 'carry out the manager's' so you write:

| 0 | *carry out the manager's* |

Write **only the missing words** on the separate answer sheet.

---

31   How many cars can this company produce in a month?

by

How many cars can .... in a month?

32   'That's the last time I talk to him!' Geoff said.

again

'I'm not going .... !' Geoff said.

33   While I was on holiday, a lot of interesting things happened to me.

my

During .... a lot of interesting experiences.

34   It was careless of you to leave without locking the door.

ought

You .... the door before you left.

35 'Is Pete likely to change his mind?' Rob asked.

chance

'Is there .... changing his mind?' Rob asked.

36 Paul is the only person who has replied to the invitation.

nobody

Apart .... replied to the invitation.

37 Are you familiar with his teaching style yet?

used

Have you .... his teaching style yet?

38 It was such a sunny day that none of us wanted to do any work.

felt

None of us .... any work because it was such a sunny day.

39 Barbara couldn't sing or dance.

unable

Besides .... , Barbara couldn't dance either.

40 Dinner will be served immediately upon our arrival at the hotel.

soon

Dinner will be served .... at the hotel.

Visual materials for Paper 5

1A

1B

1E

C3

1C

1D

2A

2B

2E

2C

2D

3A

3B

3E

3C

3D

4A

4B

4E

4C

4D

Part 4

For questions **41-55**, read the text below and look carefully at each line. Some of the lines are correct, and some have a word which should not be there.

If a line is correct, put a tick (✓) by the number **on the separate answer sheet**. If a line has a word which should **not** be there, write the word **on the separate answer sheet**. There are two examples at the beginning (**0** and **00**).

Examples:

0	*am*
00	✔

REPORT ON AN ENGLISH LANGUAGE COURSE

0	In July of this year I am spent one month on an intensive English
00	language course in Melchester, in the north of England. The course
41	was held place in a modern building which was equipped with a
42	new language laboratory and a library. There were being also
43	good sports facilities. Lessons began at 9.00 in every morning and
44	have finished at 12.00. There was an hour's lunch break, after
45	which we had the choice of working in the library, by going on
46	a visit to somewhere of interest in Melchester or joining one
47	of the optional afternoon classes. The class I went to which was
48	the Business English course, and I would say that it had certainly
49	helped me to write either letters and reports in English. Every
50	weekend, excursions there were arranged to other parts of Britain,
51	including a long weekend in York, which it was very enjoyable
52	despite of the poor weather. The month was certainly useful
53	not only because my spoken English having improved, but also
54	because I learned too many things about English life and culture.
55	Everyone who uses English in his or her work would benefit from this course.

Part 5

For questions **56-65**, read the text below. Use the word given in capitals at the end of each line to form a word that fits in the space in the same line. There is an example at the beginning (**0**). Write your answers **on the separate answer sheet**.

Example: | **0** | *extremely* |

THE LONDON UNDERGROUND MAP

The London Underground map is **(0)** *extremely*. well designed.   **EXTREME**

Simple, easy to understand and **(56)** ..... , it performs its primary task of   **ATTRACT**

guiding both inhabitants and **(57)** ..... round the underground system in London   **TOUR**

very well. The man behind this great **(58)** ..... was called Henry Beck,   **ACHIEVE**

an **(59)** ..... of the London Underground Drawing Office, who designed the   **EMPLOY**

map in 1931. The design of the map showed great **(60)** ..... because it   **ORIGINAL**

represented a complex network of **(61)** ..... clearly. This design was   **COMMUNICATE**

later used by most of the world's underground systems.

The map used before 1931 was messy and **(62)** ..... . So Beck decided to   **CLEAR**

sketch out a better one using a diagram rather than a **(63)** ..... map. This new   **TRADITION**

map was an enormous **(64)** ..... with the public when, in 1933, it made its first   **SUCCEED**

(65) ..... on underground platforms and at station entrances.   **APPEAR**

PAPER 4   LISTENING (approximately 40 minutes)

Part 1

You will hear people talking in eight different situations. For questions **1-8**, choose the best answer (**A**, **B** or **C**).

---

1   You overhear a man talking about an experience he had at an airport.
    What did he lose?

   A   his passport

   B   his wallet

   C   a piece of luggage

2   You hear an advertisement on the radio.
    What is special about the *Fretlight* guitar?

   A   It plays recorded music.

   B   It teaches you how to play.

   C   It plugs into a computer.

3   You hear part of a radio programme.
    What is the presenter talking about?

   A   food safety

   B   meal times

   C   healthy recipes

4   You hear two people discussing a type of pollution.
    What do the speakers agree about?

   A   the best way to solve the problem

   B   how they feel about this type of pollution

   C   how they reacted to the solution they saw

5 You hear a conversation between a shop assistant and a
customer about a compact disc.
What was the cause of the problem?

   A The customer gave the wrong number.

   B A mistake was made on the order form.

   C The disc was incorrectly labelled.

6 You overhear a conversation at a football game.
What does the speaker say about his team?

   A They're better than usual.

   B They're as good as he expected.

   C They tend to be unlucky.

7 You overhear a schoolgirl talking to her friend.
What does she think about her new teacher?

   A He is clever.

   B He is funny.

   C He is interesting.

8 In a hotel you overhear a conversation.
Who is the woman?

   A a tour guide

   B a tourist

   C a hotel receptionist

Part 2

You will hear part of a radio interview with a swimming instructor. For questions **9-18**, complete the sentences.

Paul works at a hotel in the [**9**]

He started his job in [**10**]

He particularly likes meeting [**11**] there.

Paul isn't interested in teaching [**12**]

According to Paul, [**13**] of all adults can't swim.

Paul's students are afraid of going [**14**]

His students have to put their faces into a salad bowl and [**15**]

below the surface.

The first thing they do in the pool is to [**16**]

in the water with their faces down.

Paul thinks it's essential to be [**17**] in the water.

Most people learn to swim after about [**18**]

Part 3

You will hear part of a radio programme called *Morning Market*. Five listeners have telephoned the programme because they have something to sell. For questions **19-23**, choose which of the statements (**A-F**) matches the reason each of the people gives for selling their possession. Use the letters only once. There is one extra letter which you do not need to use.

A I didn't enjoy using it.

Speaker 1   **19**

B I made a mistake.

Speaker 2   **20**

C It's an unwanted prize.

Speaker 3   **21**

D It takes up too much space.

Speaker 4   **22**

E I've got something better.

Speaker 5   **23**

F I have health problems.

Part 4

You will hear a radio interview with Peter Manson about the job he does for a record company. For questions **24-30**, decide which of the statements are TRUE and which are FALSE. Write **T** for **TRUE** or **F** for **FALSE**.

24   In the 1980s, record companies could not find new musicians.

| | 24 |

25   Peter's job is difficult because most young artists are shy.

| | 25 |

26   Peter was unwilling at first to give a contract to the band he saw in a tent.

| | 26 |

27   Some bands send him expensive presents.

| | 27 |

28   He was forced to listen to a tape containing threats.

| | 28 |

29   He tends to spend only a short time at a show.

| | 29 |

30   He signed a contract with one band without hearing them sing.

| | 30 |

PAPER 5   SPEAKING (14 minutes)

You take the Speaking test with another candidate, referred to here as your partner. There are two examiners. One will speak to you and your partner and the other will be listening. Both examiners will award marks.

Part 1 (3 minutes)

The examiner asks you and your partner questions about yourselves. You may be asked about things like 'your home town', 'your interests', 'your career plans', etc.

Part 2 (4 minutes)

The examiner gives you two photographs and asks you to talk about them for one minute. The examiner then asks your partner a question about your photographs and your partner responds briefly.

Then the examiner gives your partner two different photographs. Your partner talks about these photographs for one minute. This time the examiner asks you a question about your partner's photographs and you respond briefly.

Part 3 (approximately 3 minutes)

The examiner asks you and your partner to talk together. You may be asked to solve a problem or try to come to a decision about something. For example, you might be asked to decide the best way to use some rooms in a language school. The examiner gives you a picture to help you but does not join in the conversation.

Part 4 (approximately 4 minutes)

The examiner joins in the conversation. You all talk together in a more general way about what has been said in Part 3. The examiner asks you questions but you and your partner are also expected to develop the conversation.

Test 4

PAPER 1   READING (1 hour 15 minutes)

Part 1

You are going to read a magazine article about a sport called paragliding. Choose the most suitable heading from the list **A-I** for each part (**1-7**) of the article. There is one extra heading which you do not need to use. There is an example at the beginning (**0**).

Mark your answers **on the separate answer sheet**.

   A   Repetitive flights

   B   Thoughts at the top of the mountain

   C   Discovering the secret

   D   A nervous landing

   E   Floating above

   F   Some personal attention

   G   Heading for the take-off site

   H   Obeying the command

   I   An interest in a new sport

Fly like an Eagle

In the first report in our special feature on ACTIVITY HOLIDAYS WITH A DIFFERENCE, Anna Wootton takes to the air to experience the pleasures of paragliding.

0	I

A number of years ago, I'd seen bright-coloured wings in the air while on a skiing holiday in Chamonix, France. I soon found out what they were and how to go about learning this new mountain sport of 'paragliding'. When I went to live there a year later, I enrolled on the first available course at the local school.

1	

The first of the five days of instruction is spent in a field learning the characteristics of the wing and everything which goes with it. Having spent some time untangling lines and preparing to take off, you are then ready to puff out the wing. You soon find out that forcing it does not work and that there is a technique to putting air into the cells, allowing the wing to rise above your head. This launch technique is practised again and again to teach you the importance of a clean take-off, as this is where the majority of accidents occur.

2	

The following day is again spent practising blowing up the wing, but this time on a small hill. Applying the techniques, you take off and fly about 100 metres, then land gently below. Flying, landing, collecting the wing over your shoulder and walking back up the hill become exhausting, but eventually everything starts to come together. Your ability and confidence rise until you are informed that all the course students are ready to make their first major flight.

3	

After a restless night, you rise to peer up at the mountain, knowing that today you are going to launch yourself off it. You feel sick as you take the lift up. With a dry mouth you mentally rehearse all that you've been taught. You don't want to admit it, but you're scared. However, you also know that you have got this far and there is no way that you are going to back out.

4	

At 1,000 metres above the town, which now looks very small below, you certainly have doubts about why you are here. No-one in your group is pushing to go first; everyone takes their time laying out their wings and preparing to fly. Having checked and rechecked everything, you put your helmet on, switch on the radio and strap yourself in.

5	

Your turn comes and your instructor does a final check that all the lines are in the correct positions. Then he calmly informs you that he will stand directly in front, with his back to the wind, and when everything is right he will count to three and you are to run directly at him.

6	

'OK, on me, 1 ... 2 ... 3 ... go!!!' This is the last instruction you hear with your feet still on the ground. You run forward, you feel the lines tighten and the pull of the wing as it rises above your head. You correct its balance and keep running off the side of the mountain. The wing lifts you and the mountain drops dramatically away.

7	

On your first flight, you don't seem to get a chance to take in the view. You dare not move, but you do realise the expanse of air between you and the ground over 1,000 metres below. And everything is silent except for the wonderful sound of the air rushing through your helmet.

Part 2

You are going to read an article in which a film critic talks about his work. For questions **8-15**, choose the answer (**A**, **B**, **C** or **D**) which you think fits best according to the text.

Mark your answers **on the separate answer sheet**.

Film Critic

Mark Adams looks back over the last ten years of his work
as a film critic for a newspaper called *The Front Page*.

Writing articles about films for *The Front Page* was my first proper job. Before then I had done bits of reviewing – novels for other newspapers, films for a magazine and anything I was asked to do for the radio. That was how I met Tom Seaton, the first arts editor of *The Front Page*, who had also written for television. He hired me, but Tom was not primarily a journalist, or he would certainly have been more careful in choosing his staff.

At first, his idea was that a team of critics should take care of the art forms that didn't require specialised knowledge: books, TV, theatre, film and radio. There would be a weekly lunch at which we would make our choices from the artistic material that Tom had decided we should cover, though there would also be guests to make the atmosphere sociable.

It all felt like a bit of a dream at that time: a new newspaper, and I was one of the team. It seemed so unlikely that a paper could be introduced into a crowded market. It seemed just as likely that a millionaire wanted to help me personally, and was pretending to employ me. Such was my lack of self-confidence. In fact, the first time I saw someone reading the newspaper on the London underground, then turning to a page on which one of my reviews appeared, I didn't know where to look.

Tom's original scheme for a team of critics for the arts never took off. It was a good idea, but we didn't get together as planned and so everything was done by phone. It turned out, too, that the general public out there preferred to associate a reviewer with a single subject area, and so I chose film. Without Tom's initial push, though, we would hardly have come up with the present arrangement, by which I write an extended weekly piece, usually on one film.

The luxury of this way of working suits me well. I wouldn't have been interested in the more standard film critic's role, which involves considering every film that comes out. That's a routine that would make me stale in no time at all. I would soon be sinking into my seat on a Monday morning with the sigh, 'What insulting rubbish must I sit through now?' – a style of sigh that can often be heard in screening rooms around the world.

The space I am given allows me to broaden my argument – or forces me, in an uninteresting week, to make something out of nothing. But what is my role in the public arena? I assume that people choose what films to go to on the basis of the stars, the publicity or the director. There is also such a thing as loyalty to 'type' or its opposite. It can only rarely happen that someone who hates westerns buys a ticket for one after reading a review, or a love story addict avoids a romantic film because of what the papers say.

So if a film review isn't really a consumer guide, what is it? I certainly don't feel I have a responsibility to be 'right' about a movie. Nor do I think there should be a certain number of 'great' and 'bad' films each year. All I have to do is put forward an argument. I'm not a judge, and nor would I want to be.

8 What do we learn about Tom Seaton in the first paragraph?

   A He encouraged Mark to become a writer.
   B He has worked in various areas of the media.
   C He met Mark when working for television.
   D He prefers to employ people that he knows.

9 The weekly lunches were planned in order to

   A help the writers get to know each other.
   B provide an informal information session.
   C distribute the work that had to be done.
   D entertain important visitors from the arts.

10 When Mark first started working for *The Front Page*, he

   A doubted the paper would succeed.
   B was embarrassed at being recognised.
   C felt it needed some improvement.
   D was surprised to be earning so much.

11 What does Mark mean when he says that Tom's scheme 'never took off' (line 31)?

   A It was unpopular.
   B It wasted too much time.
   C It wasn't planned properly.
   D It wasn't put into practice.

12 In the end, the organisation of the team was influenced by

   A readers' opinions.
   B the availability of writers.
   C pressure of time.
   D the popularity of subjects.

13 Why does Mark refer to his way of working as a 'luxury' (line 40)?

   A He can please more readers.
   B He is able to make choices.
   C His working hours are flexible.
   D He is able to see a lot of films.

14 In Mark's opinion, his articles

   A are seldom read by filmgoers.
   B are ignored by stars and film directors.
   C have little effect on public viewing habits.
   D are more persuasive than people realise.

15 Which of the following best describes what Mark says about his work?

   A His success varies from year to year.
   B He prefers to write about films he likes.
   C He can freely express his opinion.
   D He writes according to accepted rules.

Part 3

You are going to read a newspaper article about a dentist. Eight sentences have been removed from the article. Choose from the sentences **A-I** the one which fits each gap (**16-22**). There is one extra sentence which you do not need to use. There is an example at the beginning (**0**).

Mark your answers **on the separate answer sheet**.

Fun at the Dentist's?

If you walk into W. Lloyd Jerome's dental surgery in Glasgow, you'll see bright paintings and a fashionable blue couch which patients sit on while he checks their teeth. Jerome says, ' **0** **I** That's because they're frightened.'

He has tried to create an environment where people are not afraid. ' **16** I find that's one of the things that people associate with pain. In fact, my philosophy is that dental treatment should take place in an atmosphere of relaxation, interest and, above all, enjoyment.'

Which is all highly shocking for anyone (most of us) who associates dental treatment with pain, or at the very least, formal, clinical visits. He says, ' **17** '

Virtual-reality headsets are one of his new relaxation techniques. ' **18** The headsets are used for the initial check-up, where the patient sits on the blue couch and watches an underwater film while I look at their teeth. Then the headset switches to a special camera, to give the patient a visual tour around their mouth.'

Another key point is that the surgery smells more like a perfume shop than a dentist's. Today there is the smell of orange. ' **19** Smell is very important. That dental smell of surgical spirit can get the heart racing in minutes if you're frightened of dentists.'

Known as Glasgow's most fashionable dentist, Jerome is keen to point out that he takes his work very seriously. ' **20** '

For example, Jerome uses a special instrument which sprays warm water on the teeth to clean them, rather than scraping them. ' **21** '

Five years ago, Jerome went to the United States to do research. ' 22 ' He sees his patient-centred attitude as the start of a gradual movement towards less formality in the conservative British dentistry profession.

At that moment, a patient arrives. Jerome rushes over, offers him a cup of tea (herbal or regular), asks him what video he'd like to watch and leads him gently towards the chair.

A One of the things I found out there was that when you make it easier for the patient, you make it easier for yourself.

B That's why I don't wear a white coat.

C If people are relaxed, entertained and correctly treated, they will forget such previous negative experiences.

D The relaxation techniques are important but the quality of the treatment is the most important thing.

E We were the first practice in Britain to introduce them.

F It feels a bit strange, but as long as people are relaxed, it's not painful.

G Now they look forward to their visits here.

H When people walk in, I want them to realise with all their senses that it's not like going to the dentist's.

I Fifty per cent of the population only go to the dentist when they're in pain.

Part 4

You are going to read a magazine article about theme parks in Britain. For questions **23-35**, choose from the theme parks (**A-E**). The theme parks may be chosen more than once. There is an example at the beginning (**0**).

Mark your answers **on the separate answer sheet**.

Of which theme parks are the following stated?

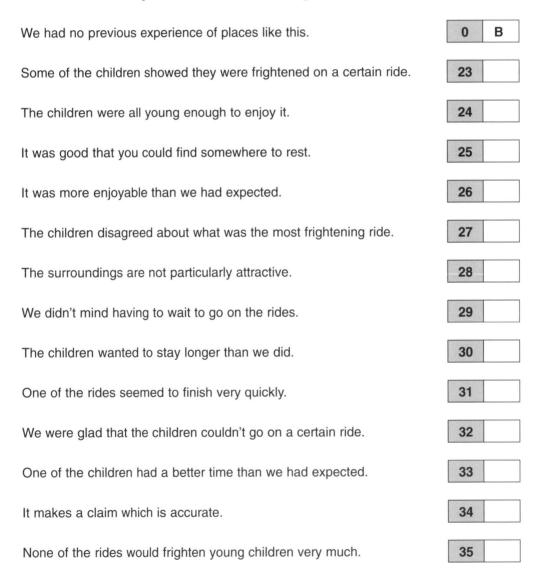

We had no previous experience of places like this.	0	B
Some of the children showed they were frightened on a certain ride.	23	
The children were all young enough to enjoy it.	24	
It was good that you could find somewhere to rest.	25	
It was more enjoyable than we had expected.	26	
The children disagreed about what was the most frightening ride.	27	
The surroundings are not particularly attractive.	28	
We didn't mind having to wait to go on the rides.	29	
The children wanted to stay longer than we did.	30	
One of the rides seemed to finish very quickly.	31	
We were glad that the children couldn't go on a certain ride.	32	
One of the children had a better time than we had expected.	33	
It makes a claim which is accurate.	34	
None of the rides would frighten young children very much.	35	

Variations on a Theme

If you're thinking of taking children to a theme park, there are dozens to choose from in Britain. We asked five families to test the best.

A Fun Island

Jan and Steve Burns took daughter Samantha, 3, and her cousins Gary, 8, and Jemma, 10.

Last year we went to a huge theme park in the US and we thought that Fun Island might seem dull by comparison. In fact, we were impressed. The park tries hard to cater for younger children, so our three-year-old didn't feel left out. The kids all loved the Crocodile Ride and the Giant Wheel. There's a special dodgems ride for the very young kids, which was a great success. For older children, there are scarier rides, such as Splash Out, where you end up jumping in a pool! After five hours, Steve and I were ready to call it a day, but the children objected because they were having such fun. Our only criticism would be that the park is slightly lacking in atmosphere, and the scenery leaves something to be desired. But the staff are extremely helpful and we felt it was clean, well organised and very security-conscious.

B Wonderland

Moira McMillan and her friend Frances took Oscar, 18 months, Ellie, 4, Alex, 5, and Alexander, 6.

None of us had been to a theme park before, so we didn't know what to expect. We thought Oscar might be too young, but he adored it. He was in heaven on the Mountain Train, and particularly liked Little Land, with its small replicas of famous buildings that were at his level! The older children enjoyed the ferris wheel, and loved driving the toy cars on a proper road layout. We spent six hours there and were glad that there were places where you could put your feet up. The landscaping is perfect and the staff very helpful and friendly. And there's something for everyone, adults included.

C Adventure World

Tim Jeffree and his wife Clare took Timothy, 3, Olivia, 7, and Emma, 9.

After seven hours we felt there was still a lot to see. This is an enormous theme park, extremely well run and full of good rides. The children love the Big Top Circus, which had a fantastic trapeze act and kept us on the edge of our seats. We went on the Terror Line and, although the girls were rather scared and kept their eyes shut most of the time, they said they'd enjoyed it. Their favourite ride was Running River, where you think you're going to get soaked, but you don't. For younger children, Toy Land is great fun. The children had a look at the new ride, Fear Factor, but we breathed a sigh of relief when they found that they were too small to go on it! The park is so well designed that even queuing for rides isn't too boring. It's spotlessly clean, and the staff are great. On one ride I couldn't sit with both girls, so a member of staff offered to go with one of them.

D The Great Park

Jenny Langridge and her friend Linda took Ben, 6, James, 9, and Sophie, 12.

We arrived at one o'clock and were disappointed that the park was only open until 5 p.m. This is a super theme park for younger children because the rides aren't too terrifying. I'm a real coward but even I enjoyed myself. We all adored Exotic Travels, a boat ride which starts off quite tamely and then becomes terrific fun. We queued for half an hour for Lightning River, and then it was over before we knew it! I wouldn't go on the Big Leap, but if you have the nerve, it looked great. There are lots of enjoyable boat and train trips around the park and I felt all the attractions were very safe and well controlled. If the children had been a little older, they might have found it a bit tame, but they were all in the right age group and they loved it.

E Fantasy World

Bill Breakall and his wife Ruth took Sarah, 10, Tom, 13, Jennie, 15, and Ben, 19.

According to the park's advertising there is 'No Limit to the Fun', and we certainly felt that was true. Europe's tallest roller-coaster, the Rocket, dominates the skyline, and Ben thought it was the most terrifying of the rides, although Jennie said the Hanger, where you hang upside-down 30 metres above the ground, was even worse! There are a dozen or so main rides, which the older children went on several times. Sarah was too small for a couple of them, but enjoyed the Long Slide. Tom loved the zoo and wildlife park. The park is clean and has good parking facilities. We found the staff attitudes were mixed. Some of them were great with the younger children, but the welcome wasn't always as warm. You need a full day to enjoy Fantasy World. We wouldn't have dared tell the kids we were going home early.

PAPER 2   WRITING (1 hour 30 minutes)

Part 1

You **must** answer this question.

1   Your English class is going to spend three days in London. The Principal of your college, Mr Robertson, has already organised the programme.

However, the students in your class have seen an advertisement for the *London Fashion and Leisure Show* and you would all like to go to the show. Your class has asked you to write to Mr Robertson about this. Read the extract from Mr Robertson's programme, the advertisement and your notes. Then, using the information, write a letter to Mr Robertson.

Monday 13 March
Morning: Sightseeing by bus
Afternoon: River trip to Greenwich

Tuesday 14 March
Morning: Science Museum
Afternoon: Shopping

Wednesday 15 March
Morning: National Art Gallery
Afternoon: Free time

THE LONDON FASHION AND LEISURE SHOW

Central Exhibition Hall, London
Tuesday March 14
10.00 – 19.00

• Latest fashions
• Leisure and sports wear
• Make-up
• Hairstyles

Students: free!

Notes

• *Thanks – good programme, especially ...*
• *Explain about London Fashion and Leisure Show*
• *Great opportunity because ...*
• *Suggest how programme could be changed*

Write a **letter** of between **120** and **180** words in an appropriate style on the opposite page. Do not write any postal addresses.

Question 1

....
....
....
....
....
....
....
....
....
....
....
....
....
....
....
....
....
....
....
....
....
....
....
....
....
....
....
....
....

Part 2

Write an answer to **one** of the questions **2-5** in this part. Write your answer in **120-180** words in an appropriate style on the opposite page. Put the question number in the box.

2   After a class discussion on the media's treatment of famous people, your teacher has asked you to write a composition, giving your opinions on the following statement:

Famous people, such as politicians and film stars, deserve to have a private life without journalists following them all the time.

Write your **composition**.

3   You see this announcement in an international magazine.

We invite you, our readers, to write an article on:

The Home of the Future

In what ways do you think people's homes will be different in the future?

In what ways might they still be the same?

The writer of the best article will win a prize.

Write your **article**.

4   Your English teacher has asked you to write a story for the college magazine. Your story must **begin** with these words:

It was dangerous, but I knew I had to do it.

Write your **story**.

5   Answer **one** of the following two questions based on your reading of **one** of these set books. Write (**a**) or (**b**) as well as the number **5** in the question box, and the **title** of the book next to the box. Your answer **must** be about one of the books below.

Best Detective Stories of Agatha Christie – Longman Fiction
The Old Man and the Sea – Ernest Hemingway
A Window on the Universe – Oxford Bookworms Collection
Cry Freedom – John Briley
Wuthering Heights – Emily Brontë

Either   (a)   Your teacher has asked you to write a composition, giving your opinions on the following statement:

A good book should interest, amuse or teach the reader something.

Write your **composition**, explaining your views with reference to the book or one of the short stories you have read.

Or   (b)   Your pen friend has written to ask you whether the book you have read would be a suitable present for her cousin's fifteenth birthday. Write a letter to your pen friend, giving your opinion with reference to the book or short story you have read.

Write your **letter**.

Question

PAPER 3   USE OF ENGLISH (1 hour 15 minutes)

Part 1

For questions **1-15**, read the text below and decide which answer (**A**, **B**, **C** or **D**) best fits each space. There is an example at the beginning (**0**).

Mark your answers **on the separate answer sheet**.

Example:

0   A   recommended   **B**   reminded   **C**   recognised   **D**   remembered

A FAMOUS EXPLORER

Captain James Cook is **(0)** ..... today for being one of Britain's most famous explorers of the 18th century. Cook was **(1)** ..... most other explorers of the same period as he did not come from a wealthy family and had to work hard to **(2)** ..... his position in life. He was lucky to be **(3)** ..... by his father's employer, who saw that he was a bright boy and paid for him to attend the village school. At sixteen, he started **(4)** ..... in a shop in a fishing village **(5)** ..... on the coast and this was a turning **(6)** ..... in his life. He developed an interest in the sea and eventually joined the Royal Navy **(7)** ..... to see more of the world.

Cook was **(8)** ..... by sailing, astronomy and the production of maps, and quickly became an expert **(9)** ..... these subjects. He was also one of the first people to **(10)** ..... that scurvy, an illness often suffered by sailors, could be prevented by careful **(11)** ..... to diet. It was during his **(12)** ..... to the Pacific Ocean that Cook made his historic landing in Australia and the **(13)** ..... discovery that New Zealand was two **(14)** ..... islands. He became a national hero and still **(15)** ..... one today.

1 **A** different   **B** contrary   **C** distinct   **D** unlike

2 **A** manage   **B** succeed   **C** achieve   **D** fulfil

3 **A** remarked   **B** viewed   **C** glanced   **D** noticed

4 **A** trade   **B** work   **C** career   **D** job

5 **A** held   **B** placed   **C** positioned   **D** situated

6 **A** moment   **B** instant   **C** point   **D** mark

7 **A** in view   **B** in order   **C** as   **D** due

8 **A** keen   **B** eager   **C** fascinated   **D** enthusiastic

9 **A** from   **B** over   **C** in   **D** for

10 **A** regard   **B** estimate   **C** catch   **D** realise

11 **A** attention   **B** organisation   **C** observation   **D** treatment

12 **A** travel   **B** voyage   **C** excursion   **D** tour

13 **A** serious   **B** superior   **C** major   **D** leading

14 **A** shared   **B** particular   **C** common   **D** separate

15 **A** keeps   **B** stands   **C** maintains   **D** remains

Part 2

For questions **16-30**, read the text below and think of the word which best fits each space. Use only **one** word in each space. There is an example at the beginning (**0**).
Write your answers **on the separate answer sheet**.

Example: | **0** | *one* |

INDOOR CLIMBING

Rock climbing is (**0**) ...*one*... of the UK's fastest growing sports. Nowadays, however, it's not necessary to head to the hills when you decide to (**16**) .... it up as a hobby. Indoor climbing is a great way to discover whether or (**17**) .... you have a head for heights. Whatever you may have (**18**) .... told, size and strength aren't that important in climbing. Climbers just (**19**) .... to be fit, with a good sense of balance. Man-made climbing walls have footholds and handholds (**20**) .... different shapes and sizes. Beginners can choose walls with holds near to (**21**) .... other. More difficult routes up the wall will have small handholds quite (**22**) .... apart.

Climbers work in pairs. (**23**) .... one person climbs, the other one stays on the ground, giving out the rope. You (**24**) .... taught to move your hands and feet correctly, plus how to rest and balance (**25**) .... the way up. Once you've mastered all of (**26**) .... basic moves, you can go for longer climbs. The great thing about climbing is that you can (**27**) .... better quite quickly. Most sports centres will include the cost of hiring equipment (**28**) .... the admission price, (**29**) .... is usually between £4 and £6 per visit. It's natural to be scared at (**30**) .... , but soon you'll realise that you're quite safe!

Part 3

For questions **31-40**, complete the second sentence so that it has a similar meaning to the first sentence, using the word given. **Do not change the word given**. You must use between **two** and **five** words, including the word given.

Here is an example (**0**).

Example:

0   You must do exactly what the manager tells you.

   carry

   You must .... instructions exactly.

The gap can be filled by the words 'carry out the manager's' so you write:

0	*carry out the manager's*

Write **only the missing words** on the separate answer sheet.

---

31   My brother accused me of taking his car.

   took

   'You .... you?' said my brother.

32   That's the strangest film I've ever seen!

   strange

   I've .... film before!

33   A very friendly taxi driver drove us into town.

   driven

   We .... a very friendly taxi driver.

34   My aunt was determined to pay for our tickets.

   insisted

   My aunt .... for our tickets.

95

35 The manager failed to persuade Karen to take the job.

succeed

The manager .... Karen to take the job.

36 I'd rather you didn't use that red pen.

mind

Would .... that red pen?

37 I last saw Mark a year ago.

since

I have .... year.

38 John impressed his new boss by settling down to work quickly.

good

John .... his new boss by settling down to work quickly.

39 Tony regrets lying to his teacher.

wishes

Tony .... his teacher the truth.

40 I found it difficult to follow the instructions.

trouble

I .... the instructions.

Part 4

For questions **41-55**, read the text below and look carefully at each line. Some of the lines are correct, and some have a word which should not be there.

If a line is correct, put a tick (✓) by the number **on the separate answer sheet**. If a line has a word which should **not** be there, write the word **on the separate answer sheet**. There are two examples at the beginning (**0** and **00**).

Examples:

0	✓
00	*too*

FINLAND

0	Finland is a country in the far north of Europe. Most of it is forest
00	and there are too about sixty thousand lakes there as well. It has a population
41	of some five million people, about a million of them who living in the capital
42	city, Helsinki. There are two official languages, Finnish and Swedish,
43	with about six per cent of the population being Swedish-speaking. Many
44	people think of Finland as for a very cold country where it is dark most of
45	all the time. In the long winter, temperatures are indeed very low and in some
46	parts there is very little daylight. However, in the summer it is often hot
47	and sunny, and it hardly just gets dark at all at night. One thing that Finland
48	is famous for is the sauna. A sauna is a kind of hot steam bath. You sit in
49	a room where steam is produced out and the temperature gets very high. You
50	then wash yourself or have a swim. Some people they even roll in the snow
51	in the winter! Finland is a very much keen sporting nation and over the years it
52	has had a number of champions in any winter sports such as ski-jumping and
53	ice hockey, as well as by producing some great Olympic athletes, especially in
54	long-distance running and the javelin. Other Finns who have been gained
55	international fame include the composer, Sibelius, and the architect and designer,
	Alvar Aalto.

Part 5

For questions **56-65**, read the text below. Use the word given in capitals at the end of each line to form a word that fits in the space in the same line. There is an example at the beginning (**0**). Write your answers **on the separate answer sheet**.

Example: | **0** | *shortly* |

RUNNING ROUND THE WORLD

John Shaw will **(0)** *shortly* be setting off on a 50,000 km run,	**SHORT**
which will make him the first person to perform the **(56)** ..... act	**ORDINARY**
of running all the way round the world if he succeeds.	
His timetable includes the **(57)** ..... Russian winter and the burning	**FREEZE**
African summer. And he has no back-up team for **(58)** ..... . He will be	**ASSIST**
running alone, carrying all his **(59)** ..... on his back.	**EQUIP**
'My biggest fear is not the physical challenge, but **(60)** ..... ,' Mr Shaw	**LONELY**
said. 'I'm as sociable as anyone and I'm very **(61)** ..... that	**HOPE**
I will form many **(62)** ..... on the way.'	**FRIEND**
On a trial 2,000 km run under the blazing **(63)** ..... of the African sun,	**HOT**
he came across wild baboons and **(64)** ..... snakes, but he proved that	**POISON**
a target of 60 kilometres a day was **(65)** ..... . 'I have made up my	**REASON**
mind to do it and I will. Running is my life,' he said.	

PAPER 4   LISTENING (approximately 40 minutes)

Part 1

You will hear people talking in eight different situations. For questions **1-8**, choose the best answer (**A**, **B** or **C**).

---

1   You overhear some people talking at a party in a hotel.
Where did the people first meet each other?

   A   at school

   B   at work

   C   at a wedding

2   You overhear a conversation in a restaurant.
Why haven't they seen each other lately?

   A   He has been too busy.

   B   He has been ill.

   C   He has been away.

3   You overhear someone talking about a concert.
How did she feel at the time?

   A   angry

   B   frightened

   C   disappointed

4   You hear a writer of children's stories talking about books
and compact discs.
What advantage does he think books have over compact discs?

   A   They may last for a longer time.

   B   They are easier to look after.

   C   They contain better quality material.

5 You hear a husband and wife talking about their summer holidays.
What problem do they have?

    A   They really hate flying anywhere.

    B   They can never think of anywhere to go.

    C   They never agree about what to do.

6 You hear a researcher being asked about her work.
What is she doing when she speaks?

    A   denying an accusation

    B   disproving a theory

    C   accepting a criticism

7 You overhear a woman talking to a friend on a train.
What does the woman think of the course she has attended?

    A   It has made her feel more confident.

    B   It has made her feel less confident.

    C   It hasn't made much difference to how she feels.

8 You overhear a woman speaking on the radio.
What is she doing?

    A   complaining about something

    B   apologising for something

    C   explaining something

Part 2

You will hear a radio report about dolphins. For questions **9-18**, complete the sentences.

Dolphins have been known to protect swimmers from sharks by getting into a

	9

Dolphins and humans have

	10

of the same size.

Swimming with dolphins can help common problems like

	11

Some people think dolphins are able to recognise human

	12

Dolphins have been used to teach children to

	13

Swimming with dolphins is used as a

	14

in projects with children.

In one jaw, dolphins have as many as

	15

Dolphins can maintain a fast pace in the water for

	16

without stopping.

Dolphins make use of

	17

to find fish.

Dolphins can be caught in

	18

or damaged by pollution.

Part 3

You will hear five different people talking about the head teacher or principal of their former secondary school. For questions **19-23**, choose from the list (**A-F**) what each speaker is saying. Use the letters only once. There is one extra letter which you do not need to use.

A   She favoured the talented students.

Speaker 1		**19**

B   She prepared us for the real world.

Speaker 2		**20**

C   She encouraged us to be imaginative.

Speaker 3		**21**

D   She was ahead of her time.

Speaker 4		**22**

E   She was concerned about the environment.

Speaker 5		**23**

F   She encouraged competitiveness.

Part 4

You will hear an interview with a tour leader who works for an adventure company in Africa.
For questions **24-30**, choose the best answer (**A**, **B** or **C**).

24   Don says that most of his passengers
   A   are not students.
   B   are looking for jobs.
   C   work in conservation.

24

25   When Don first meets a group, he
   A   gives them blankets for the overnight trip.
   B   shows them where to sit on the truck.
   C   checks they have the right equipment.

25

26   Don remembers one trip when
   A   he failed to take enough food.
   B   someone made a mistake with the food.
   C   someone complained about the food.

26

27   Don oversees the domestic work because
   A   he doesn't like to lose things.
   B   it has to be done within an hour.
   C   people complain if things are dirty.

27

28   If people argue, Don says that he
   A   prefers not to get involved.
   B   separates the people concerned.
   C   asks the group for a solution.

28

29   Don says that he sometimes
   A   needs to get to sleep early.
   B   has to camp in a noisy area.
   C   tells people when to go to bed.

29

30   What does Don say about getting up?
   A   He ignores any complaints about the time.
   B   He varies his schedule according to the group.
   C   He forces everyone to be quick about it.

30

PAPER 5 SPEAKING (14 minutes)

You take the Speaking test with another candidate, referred to here as your partner.
There are two examiners. One will speak to you and your partner and the other will be
listening. Both examiners will award marks.

Part 1 (3 minutes)

The examiner asks you and your partner questions about yourselves. You may be asked
about things like 'your home town', 'your interests', 'your career plans', etc.

Part 2 (4 minutes)

The examiner gives you two photographs and asks you to talk about them for one
minute. The examiner then asks your partner a question about your photographs and
your partner responds briefly.

Then the examiner gives your partner two different photographs. Your partner talks
about these photographs for one minute. This time the examiner asks you a question
about your partner's photographs and you respond briefly.

Part 3 (approximately 3 minutes)

The examiner asks you and your partner to talk together. You may be asked to solve a
problem or try to come to a decision about something. For example, you might be asked
to decide the best way to use some rooms in a language school. The examiner gives
you a picture to help you but does not join in the conversation.

Part 4 (approximately 4 minutes)

The examiner joins in the conversation. You all talk together in a more general way
about what has been said in Part 3. The examiner asks you questions but you and your
partner are also expected to develop the conversation.

UNIVERSITY *of* CAMBRIDGE
ESOL Examinations

Candidate Name
If not already printed, write name
in CAPITALS and complete the
Candidate No. grid (in pencil).

Candidate Signature

Examination Title

Centre

Supervisor:
If the candidate is ABSENT or has WITHDRAWN shade here ▭

Centre No.

Candidate No.

**Examination
Details**

0	0	0	0
1	1	1	1
2	2	2	2
3	3	3	3
4	4	4	4
5	5	5	5
6	6	6	6
7	7	7	7
8	8	8	8
9	9	9	9

Candidate Answer Sheet: FCE Paper 1 Reading

Use a pencil

Mark ONE letter for each
question.

For example, if you think
B is the right answer to
the question, mark your
answer sheet like this:

0 A B̶ ̶D̶ E̶ F̶ G̶ H̶ I̶

Rub out any answer you
wish to change with an
eraser.

1	A B C D E F G H I
2	A B C D E F G H I
3	A B C D E F G H I
4	A B C D E F G H I
5	A B C D E F G H I

6	A B C D E F G H I
7	A B C D E F G H I
8	A B C D E F G H I
9	A B C D E F G H I
10	A B C D E F G H I
11	A B C D E F G H I
12	A B C D E F G H I
13	A B C D E F G H I
14	A B C D E F G H I
15	A B C D E F G H I
16	A B C D E F G H I
17	A B C D E F G H I
18	A B C D E F G H I
19	A B C D E F G H I
20	A B C D E F G H I

21	A B C D E F G H I
22	A B C D E F G H I
23	A B C D E F G H I
24	A B C D E F G H I
25	A B C D E F G H I
26	A B C D E F G H I
27	A B C D E F G H I
28	A B C D E F G H I
29	A B C D E F G H I
30	A B C D E F G H I
31	A B C D E F G H I
32	A B C D E F G H I
33	A B C D E F G H I
34	A B C D E F G H I
35	A B C D E F G H I

UNIVERSITY of CAMBRIDGE
ESOL Examinations

Candidate Name
If not already printed, write name
in CAPITALS and complete the
Candidate No. grid (in pencil).

Candidate Signature

Examination Title

Centre

Supervisor:

If the candidate is ABSENT or has WITHDRAWN shade here ▭

Centre No.

Candidate No.

**Examination
Details**

0	0	0	0
1	1	1	1
2	2	2	2
3	3	3	3
4	4	4	4
5	5	5	5
6	6	6	6
7	7	7	7
8	8	8	8
9	9	9	9

Candidate Answer Sheet: FCE Paper 3 Use of English

Use a PENCIL (B or HB). Rub out any answer you wish to change with an eraser.

For **Part 1**: Mark ONE letter for each question.
For example, if you think **C** is the right answer to
the question, mark your answer sheet like this:

For **Parts 2, 3, 4** and **5**: Write your answers in
the spaces next to the numbers like this:

| 0 | A | B | C | D |

| 0 | example |

Part 1

1	A	B	C	D
2	A	B	C	D
3	A	B	C	D
4	A	B	C	D
5	A	B	C	D
6	A	B	C	D
7	A	B	C	D
8	A	B	C	D
9	A	B	C	D
10	A	B	C	D
11	A	B	C	D
12	A	B	C	D
13	A	B	C	D
14	A	B	C	D
15	A	B	C	D

Part 2

		Do not write here
16		1 16 0
17		1 17 0
18		1 18 0
19		1 19 0
20		1 20 0
21		1 21 0
22		1 22 0
23		1 23 0
24		1 24 0
25		1 25 0
26		1 26 0
27		1 27 0
28		1 28 0
29		1 29 0
30		1 30 0

**Turn
over
for
Parts
3 - 5**
→

Part 3

31		31 0 1 2
32		32 0 1 2
33		33 0 1 2
34		34 0 1 2
35		35 0 1 2
36		36 0 1 2
37		37 0 1 2
38		38 0 1 2
39		39 0 1 2
40		40 0 1 2

Part 4

Do not write here

41		1 41 0
42		1 42 0
43		1 43 0
44		1 44 0
45		1 45 0
46		1 46 0
47		1 47 0
48		1 48 0
49		1 49 0
50		1 50 0
51		1 51 0
52		1 52 0
53		1 53 0
54		1 54 0
55		1 55 0

Part 5

Do not write here

56		1 56 0
57		1 57 0
58		1 58 0
59		1 59 0
60		1 60 0
61		1 61 0
62		1 62 0
63		1 63 0
64		1 64 0
65		1 65 0

UNIVERSITY of CAMBRIDGE
ESOL Examinations

Candidate Name
If not already printed, write name
in CAPITALS and complete the
Candidate No. grid (in pencil).

Candidate Signature

Examination Title

Centre

Supervisor:
If the candidate is ABSENT or has WITHDRAWN shade here ⬚

Centre No.

Candidate No.

**Examination
Details**

0	0	0	0
1	1	1	1
2	2	2	2
3	3	3	3
4	4	4	4
5	5	5	5
6	6	6	6
7	7	7	7
8	8	8	8
9	9	9	9

Candidate Answer Sheet: FCE Paper 4 Listening

Mark test version (in PENCIL)

A   B   C   D   E

Special arrangements   S   H

Instructions

Use a PENCIL
Rub out any answer
you wish to change
using an eraser.

For **Parts 1** and **3**:
Mark ONE letter for
each question.

For example, if you
think **B** is the right
answer to the question,
mark your answer
sheet like this:

For **Parts 2** and **4**:
Write your answers in
the spaces next to the
numbers like this:

Part 1

	A	B	C
1			
2			
3			
4			
5			
6			
7			
8			

Part 2

		Do not write here
9		1 9 0
10		1 10 0
11		1 11 0
12		1 12 0
13		1 13 0
14		1 14 0
15		1 15 0
16		1 16 0
17		1 17 0
18		1 18 0

Part 3

	A	B	C	D	E	F
19						
20						
21						
22						
23						

Part 4

		Do not write here
24		1 24 0
25		1 25 0
26		1 26 0
27		1 27 0
28		1 28 0
29		1 29 0
30		1 30 0

© UCLES K&J Photocopiable

108